VMware vSphere Essentials

Efficiently virtualize your IT infrastructure with vSphere

Kunal Kumar

Christian Stankowic

BIRMINGHAM - MUMBAI

VMware vSphere Essentials

First published: May 2015

Production reference: 1260515

Published by Packt Publishing Ltd.
Livery Place
35 Livery Street
Birmingham B3 2PB, UK.

ISBN 978-1-78439-875-0

www.packtpub.com

Credits

Foreword

There is no better time to learn about VMware vSphere than this moment, right now. The data center is the most important IT asset for any business. It's the place where the applications that run automate business processes and where mission-critical data is stored. A properly designed and well-operated data center will help a business to quickly adapt in a fluid market and serve their customers better and faster. On the other hand, a poorly designed and inefficient data center will burden the business with significant expenses and damage customer relationships (security breaches and outages). Well-rounded individuals who have the skills to bring efficiency to all the aspects of the data center (servers, storage, and network) will be the most valuable IT professionals today, and for years to come.

VMware vSphere began as a leading industry server virtualization platform (with connections to legacy networks and storage environments) and introduced transformative efficiency in deploying servers in the data center. Today, with NSX and VSAN, VMware vSphere has extended its powerful virtualization technology beyond servers, bringing the same transformative efficiency to all the aspects of the data center, including networking and storage. As such, VMware vSphere has become an essential platform for the modern, well-rounded data center professional.

I'm especially excited about the VMware NSX content presented in this book, a technology that is near and dear to my heart. VMware NSX, available in vSphere, will help you conquer the last frontier of the complex and inefficient data center: networking and security. NSX is like a network hypervisor that allows you to quickly create complete virtual networks with security and L2-L7 services—on top of any physical network—all with the same ease, speed, and efficiency as deploying a virtual machine.

I hope you enjoy reading this book, and sharpen your skills on the most comprehensive and industry-leading data center virtualization platform, VMware vSphere.

Brad Hedlund

Engineering Architect, Network Virtualization
VMware, Inc.

About the Authors

Kunal Kumar is an author, researcher, digital forensics expert, and a cyber crime investigator. He has a keen interest in virtualization, information security, cyber forensics, application development, and reverse engineering. Since 2008, he has been working on various projects that deal with invention and/or structuring of security models starting from small workshops to working with Corporations, NGOs and Government agencies. He has completed his MCA, which was preceded by an MS degree in Cyber law and security and is now looking at a PhD in cloud security. He has worked with many leading IT–as a Technical advisor for Dell, as a Cloud Operations Specialist for Orange Business Services, as a Technical specialist for HCL, and as a project manager in British Telecom (BT). He has acquired some international certifications namely Certified Ethical Hacker, Computer Hacking Forensics Investigator, VMware certified Professional, and CCNA, among others. He has trained more than 1,500 students on various technologies across the Indian subcontinent. He is also the founder and acting president of the non-profit cyber welfare organization Ethical Hackers League and is rigorously involved in various social welfare causes.

Currently, he heads and runs SomethingCool (`http://somethingcool.in`), where along with his team, he works on new products with just innovation as the key element. He can be reached at `http://kunalkumar.in`

I wish to thank my parents and my grandmother for their blessings that have abled me to reach this position. I also wish to thank my brother, Karan, for his endless support and motivation during the course of this project and otherwise. I owe a big thanks to my friends, especially Viren, Yachin, Ankur, Ankush, Ekta, Pooja, Nitin, Karan, Uday, Ayushi, Himani, Sanjana, Tasmin, and Hanna.

This book could not have been possible without the constant help, support, and extraordinary patience of the content development editor, Shweta Pant. Shweta, you have been a wonderful editor and an even better friend. Thank you.

Christian Stankowic has been working as a certified IT engineer for 5 years. His interest in Linux and virtualization technology started in 2006 when he gained his first experiences with openSUSE, Debian, Ubuntu, CRUX Linux, and VMware Server. Since his apprenticeship as an IT specialist for system integration, Red Hat Enterprise Linux, CentOS, Red Hat Satellite/Spacewalk, Nagios/Icinga and SUSE Linux Enterprise Server became his key qualifications. Recent VMware technologies, such as vSphere and the vCenter family, are part of his daily work as virtual infrastructure's responsible. In his free time, he works on his personal IT blog and develops web applications using recent techniques such as jQuery and PHP.

You can check out his personal blog about various IT topics at `http://www.stankowic-development.net`.

About the Reviewers

Jason Dion is a staff systems engineer at VMware. He joined VMware in 2008 and has supported enterprise accounts in Florida for most of his career that has spanned for over 20 years.

Prior to joining VMware, he was a systems engineer at Citrix, NEC, and Wyse.

He is a vExpert who holds numerous industry certifications from VMware, Citrix, Microsoft, Cisco, Compaq, and CompTIA.

You can read his blog at http://www.flcloudlabs.com or follow him on Twitter at @virtualdion or on LinkedIn at http://www.linkedin.com/pub/jason-dion/2/2b5/621.

Jason Gaudreau has over 24 years of industry experience and is currently a senior technical account manager at VMware, a leading information technology provider of enterprise application solutions. His focus is on virtualization solutions and aligning infrastructure technologies to meet strategic business objectives. He has been concentrating on data center virtualization, desktop virtualization, and building internal private clouds in a variety of technical roles over the past 10 years.

Jason has been an active blogger on virtualization since 2012 at http://www.jasongaudreau.com and can be found on Twitter at @JAGaudreau. He is honored to have been designated as a vExpert by VMware in 2013-2015 and an EMC Elect in 2014.

Before VMware, Jason was an IT architect for AdvizeX Technologies and in IT leadership at Unum Group, where he helped to develop the organization's IT strategy.

When not talking shop, he enjoys spending time with his wife, Christine, and two kids, Dylan and Tyler.

Yohan Wadia is a client-focused Virtualization and Cloud expert who has 5 years of experience in the IT industry.

He has been involved in conceptualizing, designing, and implementing large-scale solutions that are based on VMware vCloud, Amazon Web Services, and Eucalyptus Private Cloud for a variety of enterprise customers.

His community-focused involvement also enables him to share his passion for Virtualization and Cloud technologies with peers through social media engagements, public speaking at industry events, and his personal blog at www.yoyoclouds.com

He is currently working as a Cloud Solutions Engineer with Virtela Technology Services, an NTT Communications Company. He is involved with managing the company's in-house Cloud platform and works on various open source and enterprise-level cloud solutions for internal as well as external customers. He is also a VMware Certified Professional and a vExpert (2012-2013).

www.PacktPub.com

Support files, eBooks, discount offers, and more

For support files and downloads related to your book, please visit www.PacktPub.com.

Did you know that Packt offers eBook versions of every book published, with PDF and ePub files available? You can upgrade to the eBook version at www.PacktPub.com and as a print book customer, you are entitled to a discount on the eBook copy. Get in touch with us at service@packtpub.com for more details.

At www.PacktPub.com, you can also read a collection of free technical articles, sign up for a range of free newsletters and receive exclusive discounts and offers on Packt books and eBooks.

https://www2.packtpub.com/books/subscription/packtlib

Do you need instant solutions to your IT questions? PacktLib is Packt's online digital book library. Here, you can search, access, and read Packt's entire library of books.

Why subscribe?

- Fully searchable across every book published by Packt
- Copy and paste, print, and bookmark content
- On demand and accessible via a web browser

Free access for Packt account holders

If you have an account with Packt at www.PacktPub.com, you can use this to access PacktLib today and view 9 entirely free books. Simply use your login credentials for immediate access.

Table of Contents

Preface

If you ask me what has been the biggest innovation in the last 10 years in IT, I'd answer—virtualization. In comparison with legacy infrastructure designs, this has enabled IT administrators to serve applications and workloads more cost-effectively. Fulfilling flexible IT requirements was never this easy before.

VMware acts as a global player in this market; they have introduced numerous innovations in the last few years and given virtualization an enormous push. VMware dominates the server as well as the desktop virtualization market. As a result, most of the major data centers are using rock-solid VMware products to suit their customers' infrastructure needs.

This book is an introduction for those who are looking forward to benefit from the proven vSphere infrastructure. You will learn how vSphere products can assist you to implement a dynamic and scalable virtual infrastructure while reducing your infrastructure costs.

So, are you ready for the takeoff?

What this book covers

Chapter 1, *Introduction to VMware vSphere*, introduces the book by covering all the essential basics including the vSphere architecture and how it differs from its competitor's products. You will also get to know about all the major components of virtual infrastructures, such as virtual machines, CPUs, memory, networks, and storage.

Chapter 2, *VMware vCenter Server*, will introduce the vCenter Server product family and the benefits of using them. You will learn how to install, configure, and use vCenter Server to manage your virtual infrastructure.

Chapter 3, Creating Virtual Machines, covers elementary tasks that include provisioning, configuring, and using virtual machines, clones, and templates. It is designed as a step-by-step guide for new users.

Chapter 4, Managing Virtual Network, demonstrates networking concepts for virtual infrastructures, it specifically introduces virtual switches, port groups, VLANs, and advanced technologies such as load balancing.

Chapter 5, Network Virtualization with VMware NSX, focuses on VMware's most recent technology for automating network deployment and configuration tasks. By the end of this chapter, you will learn how NSX is able to address large virtual infrastructure needs and how you can deploy NSX.

Chapter 6, Managing Virtual Storage, covers essential storage concepts, such as configuring, managing, and using VMFS and NFS data stores. To top it off, the chapter also includes implementing backup and recovery using the example of vSphere Data Protection.

Chapter 7, Working with VSAN, introduces a cost-effective and efficient way to provide high-performance storage to virtual infrastructures. Especially in combination with storage policies, VSAN is able to address the most workload's requirements.

Chapter 8, Managing Virtual Machines, demonstrates various advanced virtual machine tasks that include taking snapshots and migrating and upgrading virtual machines.

Chapter 9, Resource Management and Performance Monitoring, focuses on several ways to optimize a virtual infrastructure's resources. It is designed as a step-by-step guide that will explain how you can implement resource pools, limitations, reservations. and alarms.

Chapter 10, Incorporating vSphere High Availability, Fault Tolerance, and DRS, covers major technologies to fulfill workload's availability requirements. You will also learn how to enable automatic load balancing of computing and storage resources using vSphere DRS and vSphere Storage DRS.

Chapter 11, Securing and Updating vSphere, introduces techniques to secure virtual infrastructures such as firewalls, security profiles, and vCloud Networking and Security. It also demonstrates how you can implement patch management using vSphere Update Manager.

Chapter 12, vSphere 6.0 Overview, talks about the most recent VMware product update. The chapter is a deep-dive into all technical difference in comparison with vSphere 5.5, such as virtual hardware versions, NVIDIA GRID vCPU, vCloud Air Disaster Recovery, and VSAN All-Flash.

What you need for this book

To readjust the major technologies and products in this book, you will need to have one or more hosts to install VMware vSphere. Ensure that you fulfill ESXi's hardware requirements, which are as follows:

- 64-bit x 86 CPU with at least two logical cores
- At least 8 GB memory
- At least one 1 Gbps network interface
- An SD card, a USB flash drive, or an HDD for installing ESXi
- Local hard drives for datastore or an NFS storage for advanced cluster features, such as online migrations or failover

The most standard hardware will work but VMware also offers a compatibility guide that lists tested and supported hardware components, which can be found at http://www.vmware.com/resources/compatibility/search.php.

In addition, you will also need these:

- VMware vSphere and vCenter Server installation files — you can download a 60-day trial after you register in the VMware portal at https://my.vmware.com/web/vmware/evalcenter?p=vsphere6.
- VMware Data Protection for backup and recovery scenario; this is also part of the VMware vSphere trial suite.
- At least three ESXi hosts with at least 1 additional HDD and SSD each if you want to try VSAN. When you use VSAN in production, make sure to check out VMwares Hardware Compatibility List (HCL) at http://www.vmware.com/resources/compatibility/search.php?deviceCategory=vsan.
- A Windows client for accessing both the vSphere legacy client and vSphere Web Client for management purposes. (Accessing the vSphere Web Client is also possible on Mac OS X but not on Linux.)

Who this book is for

This book is intended for administrators who aim to learn the essentials of VMware vSphere. It is sufficient to have basic understanding of virtualization concepts.

Conventions

In this book, you will find a number of styles of text that distinguish between different kinds of information. Here are some examples of these styles, and an explanation of their meaning.

Any command-line input or output is written as follows:

```
esxcli network firewall get
```

New terms and **important words** are shown in bold. Words that you see on the screen, in menus or dialog boxes for example, appear in the text like this: "Under **Manage**, select **Settings** and go to **Security Profile**".

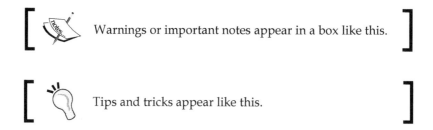

Warnings or important notes appear in a box like this.

Tips and tricks appear like this.

Reader feedback

Feedback from our readers is always welcome. Let us know what you think about this book—what you liked or may have disliked. Reader feedback is important for us to develop titles that you really get the most out of.

To send us general feedback, simply sendan e-mail to feedback@packtpub.com, and mention the book title viathe subject of your message.

If there is a topic that you have expertise in and you are interested in either writing or contributing to a book, see our author guide on www.packtpub.com/authors.

Customer support

Now that you are the proud owner of a Packt book, we have a number of things to help you to get the most from your purchase.

Downloading the color images of this book

We also provide you with a PDF file that has color images of the screenshots/ diagrams used in this book. The color images will help you better understand the changes in the output. You can download this file from `https://www.packtpub.com/sites/default/files/downloads/8750EN.pdf`.

Errata

Although we have taken every care to ensure the accuracy of our content, mistakes do happen. If you find a mistake in one of our books—maybe a mistake in the text or the code—we would be grateful if you could report this to us. By doing so, you can save other readers from frustration and help us improve subsequent versions of this book. If you find any errata, please report them by visiting `http://www.packtpub.com/submit-errata`, selecting your book, clicking on the **Errata Submission Form** link, and entering the details of your errata. Once your errata are verified, your submission will be accepted and the errata will be uploaded to our website or added to any list of existing errata under the Errata section of that title.

To view the previously submitted errata, go to `https://www.packtpub.com/books/content/support` and enter the name of the book in the search field. The required information will appear under the **Errata** section.

Piracy

Piracy of copyrighted material on the Internet is an ongoing problem across all media. At Packt, we take the protection of our copyright and licenses very seriously. If you come across any illegal copies of our works in any form on the Internet, please provide us with the location address or website name immediately so that we can pursue a remedy.

Please contact us at `copyright@packtpub.com` with a link to the suspected pirated material.

We appreciate your help in protecting our authors and our ability to bring you valuable content.

Questions

If you have a problem with any aspect of this book, you can contact us at `questions@packtpub.com`, and we will do our best to address the problem.

1
Introduction to VMware vSphere

This chapter covers all the basics of the vSphere architecture, virtualization, an introduction to hypervisors, and virtual infrastructure.

We will cover the following topics:

- Understanding the need for, and use of vSphere and how it differs from other common hypervisors
- Understanding ESXi and modes of management
- History of ESXi
- Different types of vSphere installations: Auto Deploy, fresh installation, and upgrade
- Introduction to virtual infrastructure: virtual machines, disks, CPUs, memory, switches, network, and storage

Let us start with understanding the virtualization philosophy. Virtualization is the separation of a resource or request for a service from the underlying physical delivery of that service. In other words, it's an abstraction of the operating system from hardware resources present on your server.

This blend of virtualization provides a layer of abstraction between computing, storage, and network hardware, and the application running on it. This implementation of virtualization is invisible to the end user as there is very little change to the end user experience.

The key benefit of server virtualization is the ability to run multiple operating systems on a single physical server and share the same underlying hardware resources. Virtualization has been a part of the IT industry for decades, but in 1998, VMware, Inc. delivered the benefits of virtualization to industry standard x86-based platforms.

There are two approaches to server virtualization:

- **Hosted approach**: A hosted approach provides partitioning services (virtualization) on the top of a standard operating system (for example, Microsoft Windows 7) and supports the broadest range of hardware configuration, as it uses the drivers of the underlying operating system. This design is also called **Type 2 hypervisor**. Popular products in this category are VMware Workstation and VMware Player. Comparable competitor products include Oracle VirtualBox and Parallels Desktop.

- **Bare-metal (hypervisor) architecture**: A hypervisor architecture is the first layer of software installed on a clean x86-based system. Hence, it is often referred to as the bare-metal approach. Since it has direct access to the hardware resources, a hypervisor is more efficient than hosted architectures. This enables greater scalability, robustness, and performance. VMware vSphere (ESXi) is one of the pioneers in bare-metal architecture. Bare-metal hypervisors are also called **Type 1 hypervisors**.

The following image shows differences between the two major virtualization approaches:

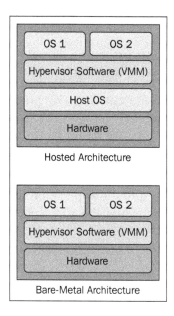

Need and use of VMware vSphere

Let us understand why a company would buy VMware vSphere. VMware vSphere consists of ESXi (the bare-metal hypervisor) and a management product named **vCenter Server**. We will be covering vCenter Server in the later chapters of the book. For now, let us focus on vSphere ESXi – the ultimate hypervisor.

The following image shows how we can expunge the disadvantages of conventional physical setups with virtualized infrastructures.

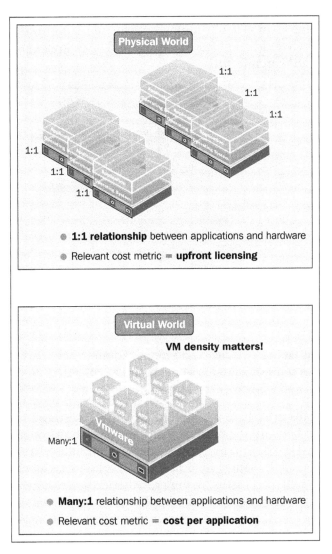

VMware ESXi is a Type 1 hypervisor that can run directly on the host server's physical hardware, without requiring an additional underlying operating system. The basic server requires some form of persistent storage (such as a hard disk or flash memory) that stores the hypervisor and supported files. It can also be run directly from the RAM of the server itself. This is called Auto Deploy setups – we will have a deeper look at this in later chapters of the book.

VMware ESXi provides the foundation for building a more reliable and dynamic IT infrastructure. This market-leading, production-proven hypervisor abstracts processor, memory, network, and storage resources into multiple virtual machines. Each virtual machine is capable of running both an operating system and its applications, as they would on physical hardware. The following image explains major parts of the ESXi architecture.

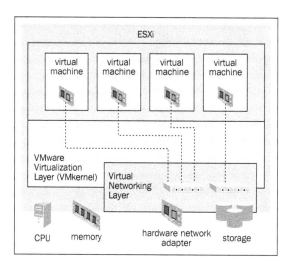

Multiple ESXi hosts can be deployed and managed more efficiently with vCenter Server. This enables centralized management and a better quality of service to data center applications and enterprise desktops.

VMware ESXi installs directly to the server hardware, inserting a robust virtualization layer between the hardware and the operating system. VMware ESXi partitions a physical server into multiple secure and portable virtual machines, that can run side by side on the same physical server. Each virtual machine represents a complete system with processors, memory, networking, storage, and BIOS. As a result, an operating system and software applications can be installed without any modification inside a virtual machine. A virtualization layer completely isolates virtual machines from each other, thus preventing a crash or configuration error in one virtual machine affecting the others.

Sharing the physical server resources amongst a number of virtual machines not only increases hardware utilization, but also decreases capital costs. The bare-metal architecture gives VMware ESXi complete control over the server resources allocated to each virtual machine. It also provides near-native virtual machine performance and enterprise-class scalability. VMware ESXi provides virtual machines with a built-in high availability, resource management, and security features to deliver improved service levels to software applications that are more efficient than static physical environments.

With the help of an example, we'll understand how a company will benefit from implementing a vSphere environment. Let's assume a company buys a server for 5,000 USD. Apart from buying the physical server, the company needs to invest in cooling (because servers generate a lot of heat), power consumption, real estate (like data center rooms), and personnel to manage that server. So all of a sudden, that physical server will cost around 6000-7000 USD, or may be even more.

Price is just one aspect of it. Let us understand the other aspect. After putting in all this money, the server utilization generally doesn't go beyond 10-15 percent annually. So, at the end of the day, the capital expenditure for the company was around 6000-7000 USD and utilization is 10-15 percent. Thus, it's a loss for the company.

Now with virtualization coming into picture, we can run multiple virtual machines on top of a single server. For example, an administrator is able to run 6 VMs on top of a physical server, with each virtual machine generating about 10 percent of resource utilization. So in total, all the virtual machines combined will generate 60 percent of resource utilization, which is far better than 10-15 percent in the previous scenario. And since virtualization helps in the consolidation of the servers, a company can save a lot by cutting down on the cost of procuring new servers.

So, cost saving and increased resource utilization are major advantages of virtualization.

Differences between VMware vSphere and other hypervisors

VMware vSphere ESXi is by far the most advanced hypervisor in the virtualization market. There are other players in the market, including Citrix, Microsoft, and Red Hat, however, VMware ESXi is the most prominent and the most feature-rich hypervisor. Let us look at how it is better and how it differs from other hypervisors present in the market:

- **Hyper-V**: Microsoft has their own server virtualization platform known as Hyper-V. It is mostly used by **Small Medium Business (SMBs)** because of lower license costs, but is gaining in market as well. It has features such as live migration, quick migration, and dynamic memory along with some other features. Microsoft Hyper-V is basically free, but as a customer you will have to buy the required Windows Server operating system. Moreover, you can buy Microsoft System Center software suite to manage a Hyper-V environment from a centralized location, but it will cost extra money.

- **XenServer**: Citrix has a virtualization platform named **XenServer**. XenServer used to be the most often used hypervisor on Linux-based systems, but lost some market segments because of more efficient alternatives such as KVM. XenServer is based on Xen, which is a free hypervisor that is also part of many Linux distributions as well. XenServer offers additional tools for easier infrastructure management (XenCenter). It is recommended that if a company is already using Citrix products, then it should consider XenServer, as they already have the expertise available from this vendor. XenServer is often used along with Citrix XenDesktop in **Virtual Desktop Infrastructure (VDI)** environments.

- **KVM**: KVM is a Linux-based open source hypervisor. First introduced into the Linux kernel in February 2007, it is now a mature hypervisor and is probably the most widely deployed open source hypervisor. KVM is used in many products, such as **Red Hat Enterprise Virtualization (RHEV)**.

The choice of hypervisor depends on the requirement. If you need a simple virtualization platform, then you can just get a free version of Hyper-V or ESXi. These two are the most popular hypervisor platforms and have really professional support, while also constantly being extended with new features. XenServer also has its advantages for those experienced in the Linux operating system.

Understanding ESXi and modes of management

There are different ways to access and work with the ESXi environment. The following topics will give us a better understanding of ESXi and its different modes of management.

History of ESXi

Prior to ESXi, VMware's hypervisor was called ESX. In comparison with ESXi, ESX had some significant differences. The most noticeable difference is that ESX's core was a highly customized Linux kernel based on Red Hat Enterprise Linux. Using a Linux user environment named Service Console, administrators used to gain privileged access to the ESX kernel. It was possible to customize ESX servers by installing additional drivers and software agents (for example, backup and monitoring) on the Service Console. The following screenshots displays the boot process of the ESX Service Console.

```
45.vmkmod succeeded.
Mounting root...kjournald starting.  Commit interval 5 seconds
EXT3-fs: mounted filesystem with ordered data mode.
ok.
100.rootfs succeeded.
Freeing unused kernel memory: 376k freed
INIT: version 2.85 booting
                VMware ESX Server 3 Service Console
                Press 'I' to enter interactive startup.
Configuring kernel parameters:                          [  OK  ]
Setting clock  (utc): Wed Apr 15 11:33:06 GMT+2 2015    [  OK  ]
Loading default keymap (de-latin1-nodeadkeys):          [  OK  ]
Setting hostname localhost.localdomain:                 [  OK  ]
Initializing USB controller (usb-uhci):                 [  OK  ]
Initializing USB controller (ehci-hcd):                 [  OK  ]
Mounting USB filesystem:                                 [  OK  ]
Initializing USB HID interface:                         [  OK  ]
Initializing USB keyboard:                              [  OK  ]
Initializing USB mouse:                                 [  OK  ]
Checking root filesystem
/: clean, 58697/640000 files, 334787/1280000 blocks
                                                        [  OK  ]
Remounting root filesystem in read-write mode:          [  OK  ]
Activating swap partitions:                             [  OK  ]
```

In 2008, the first ESXi version 3.5 was released. The versions 3.5 and 4.x were the only ones that included both ESX and ESXi variants. Beginning with vSphere 5.0, ESX was dropped by VMware to focus on ESXi. One of the disadvantages of the ESX legacy design was that it had a big footprint. Another approach for the ESXi design was to simplify management and backup functionality by outsourcing it from the kernel. As a result, ESXi is more efficient and has a much smaller footprint than ESX (at about 144 MB), enabling more dynamic vSphere environments with technologies like Auto Deploy. Many current hardware vendors are building cost-effective SD cards into their servers. Because of the low footprint, ESXi fits well on those cards, making more expensive hard drives deprecated for the ESXi operating system.

Understanding ESXi

ESXi provides a virtualization layer that abstracts the processor, memory, storage, and networking resources of the physical host into multiple virtual machines. ESXi is a bare-metal hypervisor that creates a foundation for a dynamic and automated data center.

ESXi has a very small disk footprint (about 144 MB), which adds more security, as the attack surface is very small.

In ESXi architecture, applications running in virtual machines access the CPU, memory, network, and storage without directly accessing the physical hardware present. A virtual machine consists of:

- A **virtual machine monitor** (**VMM**) process that runs inside the ESXi kernel (VMkernel). It is responsible for virtualizing the guest operating system and memory management. It also handles storage and network I/O traffic between the VMkernel and the virtual machine executable process (VMX). There is at least one VMM per virtual machine and each virtual CPU.

- A **virtual machine executable** (**VMX**) process that handles remote consoles and snapshot requests.

- A **mouse/keyboard/screen** (**MKS**) process that offers a mouse and keyboard input along with video output. Any compatible vSphere Client can connect to a VMs MKS process to control the VM console, like on physical computers.

A free version of ESXi, called vSphere free hypervisor can be downloaded from the VMware website (https://www.vmware.com/go/download-vsphere), or a licensed version of vSphere can be purchased. ESXi can be installed on a hard disk, USB device, or SD card. It can also be loaded on a diskless host (directly into memory) with a feature called vSphere Auto Deploy.

ESXi is supported on Intel processors, such as Xeon or never, and AMD Opteron processors. ESXi includes a 64-bit VMkernel. Hosts with 32-bit-only processors are not supported anymore. The last version with 32-bit support was ESX 3.5. ESXi offers support for both 32-bit and 64-bit guest operating systems.

Managing ESXi

There are two graphical user interfaces present in ESXi and vCenter Server, which can be used to interact with the vSphere environment. They are known as the VMware vSphere Web Client and the VMware vSphere client. VMware will use a modern Web Client for administration, in the future - and the legacy vSphere client (often also called **C# client**) will cease to exist in future vSphere releases. To help customers become accustomed to the new tool flavor, both clients are supported in vSphere 5.x and 6.0. Customers who are new to VMware virtualization should start with the vSphere Web Client.

The VMware vSphere Web Client is a browser based, fully extensible, platform independent administration tool for the vSphere platform. It is based on the Adobe Flex framework, and all operations necessary on VMware ESXi and vCenter Server can be undertaken using it.

The vSphere client was present in the previous versions of vSphere and is still available in vSphere 5.5 and 6.0. The vSphere legacy client is used to directly connect to ESXi hosts and also vCenter servers.

When connecting through vSphere legacy client, the following message is displayed in the client window:

In vSphere 5.5, all new features are available only through the vSphere web client. The traditional vSphere client will continue to operate, supporting the same feature set as vSphere 5.0, but not exposing any of the new features in vSphere 5.5.

The vSphere client is still used for the **vSphere Update Manager** (**VUM**), along with a few solutions (for example, site Recovery Manager and vCloud Connector).

Now we will look at different clients, which are used to manage ESXi individually.

vSphere Client

The vSphere client is one of the interfaces for managing the vSphere environment. It provides console access to virtual machines. The vSphere client is used to connect remotely to ESXi hosts and vCenter servers from a Windows system. The following screenshot shows the vSphere legacy client, connected to an ESXi host.

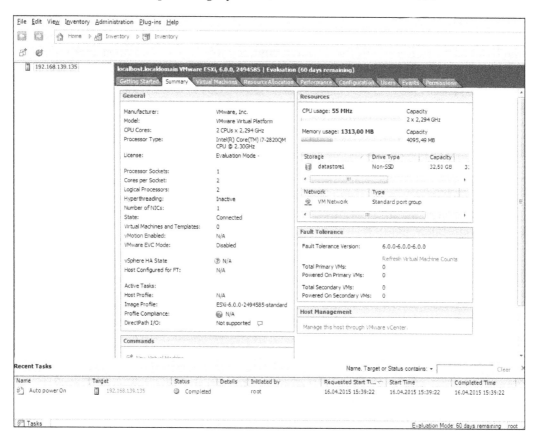

In order to connect to the vSphere environment, the administrator needs to enter the required host name, user name, and the appropriate password.

To login to the vCenter Server system with the same username and password that was used to start the windows session, we can select the **Use windows session's credentials** check box, which is optional.

vSphere Web Client

The vSphere Web Client is accessed from a browser, which can be on any operating system. As the web client still also requires Adobe Flash and Adobe dropped the support for Linux-based systems, customers need to choose between Microsoft Windows and Mac OS X for managing their virtual infrastructure. vSphere Web Client is accessed from vCenter Server directly. The application server runs a Adobe Flex client, which pulls the information from the Inventory service running on the vCenter server and shows it on the browser of the user device.

The vSphere Web Client is accessed by using a web browser. The administrator, by using the server FQDN or IP address, needs to navigate to `https://<FQDN or IP address>:9443/vsphere-client/`.

To access virtual machine consoles from the vSphere Web Client, the user needs to install a browser plugin named the VMware Client Integration Plugin. The following screenshot shows the vSphere Web Client overview.

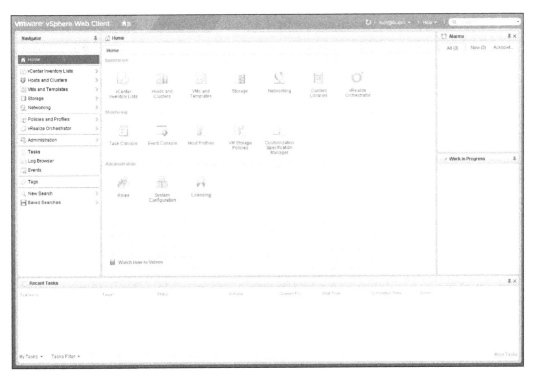

Besides the two major clients mentioned previously, there are also certain command-line tools to manage the vSphere environment from a remote location. These are:

- **vCLI**: **vSphere Command-Line Interface (vCLI)** is an application that provides a set of commands that allow us to manage ESXi hosts and vCenter servers. These commands are equivalent to those available on the ESXi shell when managing ESXi hosts using SSH or **Direct Console User Interface (DCUI)**. When a vCLI command connects through the vCenter Server system, authentication is done through the vCenter Server users and roles. Details of this will be dealt with in the later part of the book.

- **vSphere Management Appliance (vMA)**: VMware vSphere Management Assistant provides a platform for running commands and scripts for the vSphere environment. vMA is deployed as a virtual appliance that is built on SUSE Linux Enterprise Server for VMware. A virtual appliance includes one or more virtual machines that are packaged together and managed as a single unit. vMA comes with all necessary tools for managing ESXi hosts and vCenter servers, including vSphere CLI and vSphere SDK for Perl API.

- **vSphere PowerCLI**: vSphere PowerCLI is a powerful command-line tool that lets us automate all aspects of vSphere management, including network, storage, and virtual machines. It is a snap-in for Microsoft Windows PowerShell.

Virtual hardware versions

A virtual machine running on VMware vSphere is based on a particular virtual hardware version (also called virtual HW or VMHW). This version defines a list of virtual hardware and features that is available to the VM, and also defines guest operating system support. Newer vSphere versions include newer VMHW generations to enable customers to benefit from newly introduced features. VMs created on older vSphere releases can be started and customized on newer versions also, but it is not possible to run newer VMHW versions on older vSphere releases. It is also possible to upgrade the VMHW version of particular VMs to make use of newer features.

Let's have a look at some major changes between the last four VMHW versions:

Version / Feature	8	9	10	11
Compatible products	ESXi 5.0+ Fusion 4.0+ Workstation 8.0+ Player 4.0+	ESXi 5.1+ Fusion 5.0+ Workstation 9.0+ Player 5.0+	ESXi 5.5+ Fusion 6.0+ Workstation 10.0+ Player 6.0+	ESXi 6.x Fusion 7.0 Workstation 11.0 Player 7.0
Max. vRAM	1TB			4TB
Max. vCPUs	32	64		128
SATA controller	Not available		4	
Max. vDisk	2TB		62TB	

The list of differences between particular virtual hardware versions is quite long. You can look at the differences between the particular vSphere releases, in the **Configuration Maximums** documents. These documents list differences between various products and technologies including virtual machines, ESXi and vCenter Server per vSphere release:

- **vSphere 5.0**: https://www.vmware.com/pdf/vsphere5/r50/vsphere-50-configuration-maximums.pdf

- **vSphere 5.1**: https://www.vmware.com/pdf/vsphere5/r51/vsphere-51-configuration-maximums.pdf

- **vSphere 5.5**: https://www.vmware.com/pdf/vsphere5/r55/vsphere-55-configuration-maximums.pdf

- **vSphere 6.0**: https://www.vmware.com/pdf/vsphere6/r60/vsphere-60-configuration-maximums.pdf

vSphere editions and kits

VMware vSphere is available in various editions to match the customer's individual requirements. In addition, there are also two kits for smaller companies, which are looking towards starting with virtualization.

The available vSphere editions differ in their feature sets. The following table shows some of the major differences between the particular variants:

Feature / Edition	Standard	Enterprise	Enterprise Plus
Required vCenter license	vCenter Server Standard		
vMotion	Yes		Yes (including Long Distance vMotion)
Fault tolerance	Yes (2 vCPUs)		Yes (4 vCPUs)
Big data extensions	No		Yes
Distributed resource scheduler (DRS) / Distributed power management (DPM)	No	Yes	
Storage DRS	No		Yes
Storage / Network I/O Control	No		Yes
Distributed switch	No		Yes
Host profiles and Auto Deploy	No		Yes

Common features in all editions include:

- High availability
- Storage vMotion
- Data protection technology
- Hot add (adding virtual hardware resources without stopping the virtual machine; needs to be supported by the guest operating system as well)
- Storage policies

We will have a deeper look at the particular features in later chapters of this book. Enterprise plus is the most advanced but also the most expensive vSphere edition.

Customers just beginning with vSphere technology might want to have a look at the more cost-effective kits - Essentials and Essentials Plus. Both kits apply to infrastructure setups with a maximum of 3 ESXi hosts, with up to 2 physical CPUs each. While the Essentials kit only includes basic virtualization functionality, the Essentials Plus kit also includes some advanced features like the following:

- vMotion
- High availability

- Data protection
- vSphere replication

Both kits are compatible with vCenter Server Essentials. Note that the other vCenter server releases are not compatible with Essentials kits. For example, it is not possible to include an Essentials remote office in vCenter Server Standard.

Different types of vSphere installations

There are many ways to install ESXi in your environment. They are listed and discussed next.

Fresh installation

VMware ESXi requires a 64-bit server, for example AMD Opteron or Intel Xeon. The server can have up to 320 logical CPUs (cores or threads) for vSphere 5.5 and can support up to 4096 virtual CPUs per host, which requires a minimum of 4 GB of memory. An ESXi host can have up to 4TB of memory. These limitations vary depending on the vSphere release. They are listed in detail in the "Configuration Maximums" document for the particular software release.

ESXi can be installed on Flash cards, USB storage and SATA, SCSI and SAS disk drives.

To begin a fresh installation of ESXi, follow the steps listed next:

1. Insert the ESXi CD/DVD into the CD/DVD drive or attach the installer USB flash drive.
2. Restart the machine.
3. Set the BIOS to boot from the CD-ROM or USB.
4. On **Select a disk** page, select the drive on which ESXi has to be installed and press *Enter*.
5. Press *F1* to view the information of the selected disk.
6. Specify a root password for the ESXi host.

After specifying the password, ESXi will get installed on to the system. Other necessary information like the hostname, IP address, and so on, is provided after the installation, using the **Direct Console User Interface** (**DCUI**).

If booting from SAN, select the RAW LUN on which you are supposed to install the ESXi, in step 4.

Auto Deploy

Auto Deploy is a method, which enables automatic deployment of a ESXi host, which in turn increases the scalability of the vSphere environment. The reason behind this is that the administrator need not install ESXi hypervisor on all the physical hosts. Instead, vCenter Server loads an ESXi image directly onto the physical host along with the optional configuration data of the ESXi host, which is also pushed by vCenter Server. If the physical server is shut down or rebooted, then the current state of the ESXi host is lost, but the ESXi image and the configuration data is pushed back again as soon as the server is restarted. vCenter Server stores and manages ESXi updates and patching through an image profile and, optionally, the host configuration through a host profile. This setup is especially effective if you're maintaining a big amount of ESXi hosts. Instead of patching those hosts, you just need to reboot them to get the most recent ESXi image.

Upgrading an ESXi host

Upgrading an ESXi host requires VMware vSphere Update Manager, CD-ROM, or USB key installation media. vSphere Update Manager can be used to upgrade multiple ESXi hosts more efficiently in unattended mode. Before upgrading any ESXi host, make sure to create a backup of your ESXi host configuration. It is possible to do a cross platform upgrade, i.e. ESXi 4.x to ESXi 5.x. Before upgrading your environment, make sure to check the VMware Product Interoperability Matrix on the VMware website at `http://www.vmware.com/resources/compatibility/sim/interop_matrix.php`.

We will have a deeper look at the vSphere Update Manager in *Chapter 11, Securing and updating vSphere*.

Introduction to virtual infrastructure – virtual machines, disks, CPUs, memory, switches, network, and storage

Let us get a better understanding of what a virtual machine is, and how ESXi interacts with the four major components: CPU, memory, network, and storage.

Virtual machines

A **virtual machine** (**VM**) is a set of virtual hardware on which a supported guest operating system and its applications run.

A VM is also a set of discrete files. Following are some of the files that make up a virtual machine; except for the log files, all the VM files start with the VM's name (`<VM-Name>`):

1. A configuration file (`.vmx`).

2. One or more virtual disk files. The first virtual disk has files `<VM_name>.vmdk` and `<VM_name>-flat.vmdk`.

3. A file containing the virtual machine's BIOS state and configuration (`.nvram`).

4. A VM's current log file (`.log`) and a set of files used to archive old log entries (`#.log`).

5. Swap files (`.vswp`) used to reclaim memory during periods of contention.

6. A snapshot description of files (`.vmsd`). This file is empty if the virtual machine has no snapshots.

7. If the virtual machine is converted into a template, a virtual machine template configuration file (`.vmtx`) replaces the virtual machine configuration file (`.vmx`).

A virtual machine can have other files, for example, if one or more snapshots were taken or if **raw device mappings** (**RDMs**) were added. A virtual machine has an additional lock file if it resides on an NFS, iSCSI, or Fibre-channel data store. This mechanism is very important when running a cluster, to avoid VM reboots in case of network failures. In such a case, a special heartbeat connection is implemented on a datastore basis. A virtual machine has a **Changed Block Tracking** (**CBT**) file (`x-ctk.vmdk`), if it is backed up with the VMware vSphere Data Protection (VDP) appliance or compatible products. Using this technology, it is possible to detect the changed virtual hard disk blocks, and only include those in the backup processes. This speeds-up the backup dramatically, while also reducing the storage consumption of backup archives.

CPU virtualization

CPU virtualization emphasizes performance and runs directly on the available CPUs whenever possible. The underlying physical resources are used whenever possible and the virtualization layer runs instructions only when needed, to make virtual machines operate as if they were running directly on a physical machine. When multiple virtual machines are running on one ESXi host, the physical resources are shared equally by default. We will later have a look at more complex resource setups, which enable a kind of prioritization per VM basis.

vSphere's virtualization architecture is invisible to the guest operating system. There is no need to customize it to support being virtualized. Virtual CPUs can be set on a core and thread basis (for example, 2 vCPUs with 2 cores, each resulting in 4 threads available).

Memory virtualization

In a non-virtual environment, the operating system assumes that it owns all physical memory in the system. When an application starts, it uses the interfaces provided by the operating system to allocate or release virtual memory pages during the execution.

In vSphere, the ESXi kernel (VMkernel) owns all the memory resources and implements its efficiency management. VMkernel reserves some of the memory for itself; the remaining memory is available to virtual machines (including some overhead for each VM). Virtual memory is grouped into pages that are mapped into physical memory or data store resources, if the ESXi host runs out of physical memory. To avoid this scenario, vSphere offers the Ballooning functionality, which forces powered-on virtual machines to free up unneeded memory (for example, memory caches).

We will later have a deeper look at advanced memory resource management, including reservations and limitations.

Physical and virtual networking

The key virtual networking components in virtual architecture are virtual Ethernet adapters and virtual switches. A virtual machine can be configured with one or more virtual Ethernet adapters. Virtual switches allow virtual machines on the same ESXi host to communicate with each other using the same protocols that would be used over physical switches, without the need for additional hardware.

Virtual switches also support VLANs that are compatible with standard VLAN implementations from other vendors, such as Cisco. To enable more complex setups, VMware also offers distributed virtual switches that enable advanced features like **Link Layer Discovery Protocol (LLDP)** and 40GB NIC support. Distributed switches are managed centrally by vCenter Server, which reduces time and effort for network configuration.

We will have a look at more advanced network setups in later chapters.

Physical and virtual storage

Conventional file systems allow only one server to have read-write access to a file at a given time. VMware vSphere VMFS enables a distributed storage architecture that allows multiple ESXi hosts, concurrent read and write access to the same shared storage resources. VMFS is a high-performance cluster file system designed for virtual machines. VMFS uses distributed journaling of its file system metadata changes. As a result, VMFS can easily recover data in the event of a system failure. VMFS allows virtual disks to have up to 62TB capacity and also expanding storage capacity online without downtime.

Summary

In this chapter, we understood the core concept of virtualization and both, the need for and use of vSphere in infrastructure virtualization. We also had a look at the major differences between vSphere and other common hypervisors. To sum it up, virtualization is basically, abstraction of an operating system from hardware resources present on your server. In other words, it lets you install multiple operating systems on the same server, enabling the server administrator to utilize a server more effectively and efficiently. vSphere, the data center product of VMware, provides effective measures and features to create a virtual infrastructure. It can be installed on your server in three different ways – Auto Deploy, fresh installation from scratch, and upgrading over a current vSphere installation. Virtual infrastructure is made up of various components like virtual machines, disks, CPUs, memory, switches, network, and storage. It is just like a regular physical infrastructure but is managed and controlled with the help of vSphere.

In the next chapter, we will cover vCenter Server and how to import, start, and configure the vCenter Server Appliance. We will also get to know how to configure vCenter Server and how to use it to manage the server's inventory, ESXi hosts, virtual machines, and other infrastructure components. Licensing of vCenter Server and backup will also be covered in the next chapter.

2
VMware vCenter Server

In the last chapter, we discussed about various hypervisors and VMware vSphere. We understood how vSphere differs from other products, and how a virtual environment is a better choice in managing a data center. We now also know what our virtual infrastructure comprises of. So after having an introductory understanding of VMware vSphere, we will now have a look at vCenter Server and its role in VMware virtualized infrastructure.

We will cover the following topics in this chapter:

- Introduction to vCenter Server
- vCenter Server architecture
- Communication between vCenter Server and ESXi hosts
- Additional vCenter Server components
- Comparison of vCenter Server and vCenter Server Appliance
- Preparing and installing vCenter Server on Microsoft Windows
- Importing, starting and configuring the vCenter Server Appliance
- Configuring and managing vCenter Server
- Managing inventory, hosts, VMs, and templates via vCenter Server
- vCenter Server licensing
- Backing up vCenter Server

Introduction to vCenter Server

To start with, vCenter Server is the centralized management utility by VMware, and is used to manage virtual machines, multiple ESXi hosts, and all dependent components from a single centralized location. Using this tool, you're also able to take full control of advanced components including distributed switches, vMotion, Storage vMotion, templates, and clones.

vCenter Server architecture

In order to understand how vCenter Server works, it is important to understand its architecture.

The vCenter Server architecture is made up of the following components:

- **vSphere Web Client and vSphere Client**: As discussed in the previous chapter, VMware offers both vSphere Web Client and vSphere legacy client to manage ESXi hosts and virtual machines. The vSphere legacy client can be used to connect directly to an ESXi host or to vCenter Server, but vSphere Web Client is used to connect only to the vCenter Server, not individual ESXi hosts.

  - The recommendation from VMware is to use VMware vCenter Server to manage ESXi hosts and virtual machines, and therefore use vSphere Web Client, as all the new features are available only through the use of vSphere Web Client. New customers should start with vSphere Web Client in any case, as VMware plans to give up the legacy client some day.

- **vCenter Server database**: It is the most crucial component of the architecture. It stores inventory items, security roles, resource pools, performance data, and other critical information for vCenter Server. Supported databases include products like Oracle Database and Microsoft SQL Server. vCenter Server Appliance offers an integrated PostgreSQL server derivate called **vPostgres**. It is also possible to use an external Oracle Database instance, which is recommended for larger environments when using vCenter Server prior to 6.0.

- **Single Sign-On (SSO)**: vCenter SSO is used as an authentication broker and also as a security token exchange server. It therefore provides a secure way of accessing the vSphere environment. The authentication can happen against multiple user repositories known as identity sources. A detailed description on SSO will be covered in the later part of the chapter.

- **vSphere Inventory Service**: The service is used to reduce load on the main vCenter Server process as it caches client queries. Beyond that, it is responsible for managing Web Client inventory objects such as tags. Tags are very useful in bigger environments to simplify finding objects including virtual machines, data stores, clusters, and whole networks. When using multiple vCenter servers, it is possible to use vSphere Inventory Service for multiple vCenter Server instances.

- **Managed Hosts**: vCenter Server enables these to manage ESXi hosts as well as the virtual machines that run on them.

The following figure demonstrates the basic architecture of vCenter Server:

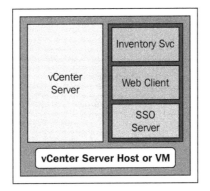

Communication between vCenter Server and ESXi hosts

The main service running on the vCenter Server is known as vpxd or VMware Virtual Server service. When an ESXi host is added to the vCenter Server, there is an agent service called vpxa, which is installed and started on the ESXi host. Vpxa acts as an intermediary service between the vpxd service running on the vCenter Server and hostd service running on the ESXi host. The hostd service running on the ESXi host is mainly responsible for managing most of the operations on the host.

It knows all the registered virtual machines, their status, and the storage volumes that are visible to the host. When commands such as creating, migrating, or suspending a virtual machine from vCenter Server is issued, the vpxd service running on the vCenter Server sends the command to vpxa, and vpxa in turn forwards it to hostd, which then executes the command.

If a command is issued through the vCenter Server, the vCenter Server database is also updated. vCenter Server is essential for managing vSphere environments, but in case of a vCenter Server failure, the other components behave like before. Virtual machines, and even advanced components like distributed virtual switches, have no permanent dependency to vCenter Server and can be used without it. If vCenter Server crashes, some features started by it, including automatic cluster load balancing (Dynamic Resource Scheduler) become unavailable.

When a vSphere legacy client is used to connect directly to the ESXi host, the communication is directly to `hostd`, and the vCenter database is not updated. This is also one of the major reasons why VMware does not recommend us to directly connect to an ESXi host and manage it.

The following figure demonstrates the process architecture of an ESXi cluster along with vCenter Server.

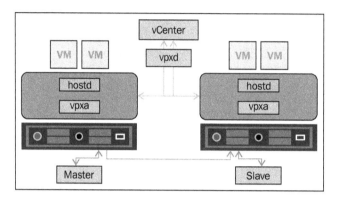

Additional vCenter Server components

vCenter Server also consists of the following services and interfaces:

- **Core services**: This includes managing resources and virtual machines, scheduling tasks, managing and generating events and alarms, and logging statistics. It also offers functionality for provisioning virtual machines and configuring hosts.

- **Distributed services**: This offers functionality for serving vSphere clusters, including (storage) vMotion, (storage) DRS, and high availability. While vMotion and storage vMotion are used for migrating virtual machines and their virtual hard disks online, DRS and Storage DRS implement automatic load balancing of computing and storage resources. vSphere high availability makes sure that virtual machines are restarted as fast as possible when an ESXi host crash happens.

- **Additional services**: vCenter Server can be integrated with additional VMware products, including vSphere Update Manager (vUM) or vCenter Orchestrator. Some additional components like vCenter Orchestrator might require a separate license. Mostly, these components are deployed as a dedicated server or appliance, and linked with vCenter Server.

- **Database interface**: This manages access to the vCenter Server database.

- **vSphere APIs**: vSphere offers a wide set of various APIs to provide interfaces for writing custom applications that access vSphere functionality. Check out the VMware website at `https://www.vmware.com/support/pubs/sdk_pubs.html` for full documentation of all provided APIs.

Comparison of vCenter Server and vCenter Server Appliance

In order to manage your virtualized data center, you are provided with some alternatives to install vCenter Server:

- Installation on a supported Windows-based operating system
- Deployment as a Linux-based virtual appliance (vCSA)

Both variants are quite similar as they both offer a wide range of management functionality, including:

- Deployment and management of virtual machines, templates, and OVF appliances
- Management of multiple ESXi hosts
- Centralized network and storage provisioning
- Statistics and performance data collection
- Advanced cluster features including DRS, high availability, and fault tolerance

Beginning with vSphere 6.0, vCenter Server and the appliance alternative have the same limitations and features. Previous versions were intended for smaller setups, as they missed support for multiple linked (Linked Mode) or clustered (vCenter Heartbeat) vCenter Server instances.

Preparing and installing vCenter Server on Microsoft Windows

vCenter Server is probably still, mostly installed on servers running Microsoft Windows. Before installing the application, it is important to ensure that all requirements are met.

Hardware, software, and network requirements

Assuming that all major vCenter Server components should be installed on one single host, the requirements are:

- 64-bit compatible processor with at least 2 logical cores and 2 Ghz
- At least 12 GB memory
- At least 100 GB hard drive capacity
- 64-bit variant of Microsoft Windows Server (2008 SP2 or newer)
- 64-bit database **Open Database Connectivity** (**ODBC**) driver and **Data Source Name** (**DSN**) for establishing database connection
- 1 GBit/s network
- Resolvable system hostname using DNS forward and reverse lookup

For alternate setup scenarios, requirements might differ. The vCenter Server documentation offers very detailed lists of recommendations and requirements for particular infrastructure scenarios.

Database preparation

In order to install vCenter Server on Microsoft Windows, you will need to install a supported database before installing the application set. Supported databases include products such as Microsoft SQL Server and Oracle Database. The VMware Product Interoperability Matrix at `http://www.vmware.com/resources/compatibility/sim/interop_matrix.php` lists all supported databases per vSphere release. Ensure that your database product is supported while planning your infrastructure setup.

vCenter Server can also be used along with a Microsoft SQL Server 2008 Express instance which is included in the installation media. As this setup is only supported for managing up to five hosts and 50 virtual machines, its primary target is to handle evaluation or very small virtual infrastructures. When using the Microsoft SQL Server express, there is no need to create a 64-bit DSN.

If you are using an external database, install the appropriate database driver and a valid 64-bit DSN. Refer to your database vendor's documentation.

vCenter Server installation

Beginning with vSphere 5.1, VMware simplified the installation process by providing a guided installation called **Easy Install** that installs all major components in their correct order:

- vCenter Single Sign-On

- vSphere Web Client

- vCenter Inventory Service

- vCenter Server

If you don't need to split the particular components on different servers, it is a very common practice to use the Easy Install method. Follow the steps listed next:

1. Accept the **End-User License Agreement (EULA)**

2. Validate network prerequisite check before proceeding to the next step. If your machine's IP address is assigned per DHCP, a warning will be displayed. It is recommended to use static IP addresses and FQDNs. Also, make sure that DNS forward and reverse lookups are working for your system, to avoid future errors.

3. Define a password for the administrator of the default SSO domain. Make sure not to lose this information, as this is the only administrator account that can be used after the installation, to manage all vCenter components.

4. Enter a SSO site name. This is especially useful if you plan to install multiple vCenter servers and SSO sites. Choose the name wisely as you cannot change this value afterwards.

5. If necessary, define an alternate HTTPS port for SSO. VMware recommends not changing the default value if possible.

6. If needed, define an alternate installation path for SSO.

7. Review and confirm the value entered.

8. Enter a license key. It is also possible to skip this and start vCenter Server in 60-days evaluation mode.

9. Select a valid DSN or the Microsoft SQL Server 2008 Express instance.

10. Pick a service user that vCenter Server will use. Per default, vCenter Server is configured to run using the Windows Local System Account. The installation utility also allows specifying a dedicated service account.

11. If necessary, change default ports for the particular vCenter components.

12. Select the size of your infrastructure. You might choose between Small (less than 100 hosts or 1000 VMs), Medium (100-400 hosts or 1000-4000 VMs), and Large (more than 400 hosts or 4000 virtual machines). The selection configures the **Java Virtual Machine** (**JVM**) memory to match your infrastructure's size.

After the installation process, vCenter Server is ready to use.

Importing, starting, and configuring the vCenter Server Appliance

When a user logs in into any of the above platforms using the vSphere client interface, he/she gets an indistinguishable difference. Because of this, the user does not come to know the platform on which the vCenter Server service is running.

The time required to deploy vCenter Server and its associated services is reduced by vCenter Server Appliance. It is also a low-cost alternative as there is no additional operating system license cost associated with VMware vCenter Server Appliance.

vCenter Server Appliance features

vCenter Server Appliance includes a prepackaged vCenter Server setup in SUSE Linux Enterprise Server 11 for vSphere operating system. It also comes with a PostgreSQL server derivate called vPostgres. For vCenter Server 5.5, this is supported by:

- Evaluating the appliance
- Managing no more than 100 ESXi hosts and 3000 virtual machines

These limitations have also changed for vSphere 6.0. The most recent release is in no way inferior to the Windows derivate anymore, giving customers the choice to use a platform best matching their individual preferences:

Feature	vCSA 5.5	vCS / vCSA 6
Hosts per vCenter	100 (1000 with external Oracle database)	1000
Registered VMs per vCenter	3000 (10,000 with external Oracle database)	15,000
Hosts per cluster	32	64
VMs per cluster	4,000	6,000
Linked mode	Not supported	Supported

vCenter Server Appliance may also be used with an external Oracle Database server setup instance. Before planning your installation, make sure to check the VMware Product Interoperability Matrix on the VMware website at `http://www.vmware.com/resources/compatibility/sim/interop_matrix.php`.

vCenter Server Appliance offers a web-based interface for configuring the appliance core configurations such as network configuration. This interface is also called **Virtual Appliance Management Infrastructure** (**VAMI**) interface. Beginning with vSphere 6.0, this has also changed, as this is also part of the vSphere Web Client. In case this is not working, there is also a shell that can be used over the virtual machine's console or the Secure Shell (SSH) remote terminal.

vCenter Server Appliance benefits

The most valuable benefit, when using the vCSA is that it requires no additional operating system license, like the Windows derivate. To install the appliance, it is sufficient to import the **Open Virtual Format** (**OVF**) template to an ESXi host. After deployment, the vCenter Server can be configured easily using a web-interface, without requiring deeper Linux administration knowledge.

The vCenter Server Appliance has the following advantages:

- It is a simplified deployment and configuration solution. The reason behind this is that it imports an appliance to an ESXi host, configures the time zone settings, and uses the web interface to configure the appliance.

- It is a low-cost alternative as there is no operating system license cost associated with VMware vCenter Server Appliance. So therefore, total cost of ownership is eliminated.

- When a user logs in using the vSphere client interface, he/she gets the same user experience as on the Windows derivate.

vCenter Server Appliance requirements

The vCenter Server Appliance empowers the server administrator to manage the virtual infrastructure with ease. However, to install it in your virtualized environment, the following requirements need to be fulfilled:

Appliance hardware	Requirements	
	vCSA 5.5	vCSA 6.0
Disk space	Minimum 70 GB Maximum 125 GB	Minimum: 86 GB Maximum: 450 GB Depending on size and deployment type (Embedded or External Platform Services Controller)
Memory allocation	Tiny: 8 GB Small: 16 GB Medium: 24 GB	Tiny: 8 GB Small: 16 GB Medium: 24 GB Large: 32 GB
Processor	2 vCPUs	Tiny: 2 vCPUs Small: 4 vCPUs Medium: 8 vCPUs Large: 16 vCPUs

VMware names the following sizes for the particular deployment types:

- Tiny: 1-10 hosts or 1-100 VMs
- Small: 1-100 hosts or 1-1000 VMs
- Medium: 100-400 hosts or 1000-4000 VMs
- Large: more than 400 hosts or 4000 virtual machines

During the appliance deployment, these values are set, to best suit your infrastructure. The VMware knowledge base offers a very detailed list of requirements and tweaks for the particular deployment scenarios:

- vCSA 5.5: http://kb.vmware.com/kb/2005086
- vCSA 6.0: http://kb.vmware.com/kb/2106572

Importing the vCenter Server Appliance

If we want to import the vCenter Server Appliance, then the following steps need to be taken:

1. Using the vSphere legacy Client, select **File | Deploy OVF Template**

2. By performing the preceding step, the appliance is imported to an ESXi host. This ESXi host is a part of the virtual infrastructure.

3. Provide the location of the **Open Virtualization Format** (**OVF**). The location can be a URL or a folder path on your local system.

4. Select a **Name and Location** for the appliance.

5. Select the datastore the appliance should be deployed on. Also select a storage provisioning type; you might choose between Thick Provision Lazy-Zeroed, Thick Provision Eager-Zeroed, and Thin Provision. While Thin Provision is supposed to be a good solution for test scenarios, as it only allocates disk capacity the vCSA uses, Thick Provisioning is more performant for production setups. Thick Provision Eager-Zeroed zeroes all reserve bits, unlike Lazy-Zeroed which only reserves the capacity needed on the storage system.

Deploying vCSA 6.0

As the vSphere legacy client will cease to exist someday, VMware offers a more modern to deploy the vCenter Server Appliance beginning with vSphere 6.0. The vCSA installation media contains an HTML page that is used along with software called the **VMware Client Integration Plugin** to deploy the appliance. Before opening the HTML page, the plugin needs to be installed.

To deploy the vCenter Server Appliance, follow the steps listed next:

1. Install the VMware Client Integration Plug-in. Its installation file is located in the `vcsa` folder on the vCSA installation media.

2. Open the **vcsa-setup.html** document in the root directory.

3. Wait for the plug-in to load and accept the access request.

4. Click **Install**.

5. Accept the End-User License Agreement (EULA).

6. Enter **FQDN** or **IP Address**, **Username**, and **Password** of the target host.

7. Assign a name for the VM, and operating system password

8. Select deployment type; we will have a deeper look at the possible scenarios later in this book. The equivalent to vCSA 5.5 embedded SSO and database setup is **Embedded Platform Services Controller**.

9. Select **Configure Single Sign-On** if you have no pre-existing SSO server in your infrastructure. Also set a SSO domain (for example, vsphere. local), site name (for example, mycompany), and the password for the SSO administrator account.

10. Assign an appliance size that fits your infrastructure best; choose between the **Tiny**, **Small**, **Medium**, or **Large** deployment templates.

11. Assign the data store the appliance will be stored on. Check **Enable Thin Disk Mode** if you want to use Thin Provision, which is often used along with evaluation scenarios.

12. Choose the integrated vPostgres database or apply valid connection settings for an external Oracle Database instance. Note that the vPostgres database is also supported for large setups in vSphere 6.0.

13. Apply network settings such as FQDN, IP address, subnet mask, gateway, and DNS servers. It is recommended that you static rather than dynamic settings. It is also sufficient to configure time synchronization; you can choose between an NTP server and the hypervisor time settings. Check **Enable ssh** if you need external terminal access to the appliance.

14. Review the settings just made and start the deployment process.

Starting the vCenter Server Appliance 5.5

Once the appliance boots, the next step is to configure the time zone. It should be kept in mind that any of the configuration settings which needs to be done for the vCenter Server Appliance, should be done from the web configuration interface or its virtual machine settings.

Configuring the vCenter Server Appliance time zone

To configure or modify the vCenter Server Appliance time zone, the following steps need to be followed for vSphere 5.x:

1. Access the appliance console.
2. Time zone is selected and the appropriate time zone of the location is set.

The default time of the vCenter Server Appliance is the synchronized time of the ESXi host on which it is running. The vCenter Server gets the 'absolute time' correct if the time synced on the user's host is properly configured.

In order to configure the vCenter Server Appliance time zone, one must follow the next steps:

1. Using the information provided in the console, a web browser and a session to the vCenter Server Appliance should be opened.
2. Go through the instructions given in the application console thoroughly and follow them to configure the minimum requirements. By doing this, the user can begin to use the appliance.

Connecting to the web interface on vSphere 5.x

Base configuration should be done the first time the user logs into the appliance. The configuration can be done through the appliance web console, and in order to do this, a web interface is present.

In order to connect to the appliance web console, one must follow the next steps:

1. Using the information provided in the console, a web browser and a session to the vCenter Server Appliance should be opened.
2. The URL used to connect to vCenter Server, using a web browser is;
   `https://<vCenterIPorFQDN>:5480`
3. Go through the instructions given in the application console thoroughly and follow them to configure the minimum requirements. By doing this, the user can begin to use the appliance.

Whenever a vCenter Server Appliance is deployed, a default password is set. This password is `vmware`. It is always advisable to change this password right after deployment, from the web console.

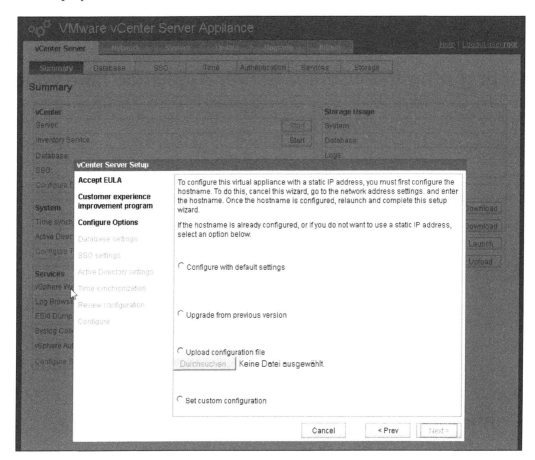

Configuring and managing vCenter Server

If the user wants to configure the appliance for the first time, he/she must first accept the EULA when using vSphere 5.x. Then, the vCenter Server Appliance is chosen and configured with the default settings. Once the settings have been saved, the appliance can be started.

Following are the steps that must be followed in order to configure the vCenter Server Appliance:

1. Accept the **End-User License Agreement (EULA)**

2. Select **Configure with Default Settings**

3. Define the database settings; select the integrated vPostgres database or apply valid connection settings for an external Oracle Database instance. Note that the integrated database is not supported for large environments in vSphere 5.5.

4. Configure SSO to deploy an embedded server or use a pre-existing SSO installation.

5. Enable Active Directory integration if applicable to your infrastructure; enter a valid domain, a username, and password, eligible to register systems.

6. Review and acknowledge the configuration settings.

After the configuration process has finished, vCenter Server is ready to use.

Managing vCenter Server Appliance services

A summary screen appears in the appliance web console. The settings for the vCenter Server Appliance can be managed from that Summary screen only.

The starting and stopping of the services can be done from here. If at all other configuration changes are to be made, they can also be done from here.

Single Sign-On

vCenter Single Sign On is a feature which was added in vSphere 5.1 software suite. It is an authentication broker and the security token exchange service, which provides a more secure way to access vSphere solutions.

What this means is that previously when a user logged into the vCenter, the authentication happened against the active directory configured for vCenter. However, since the SSO has been introduced, the user no longer needs to log into the vCenter server. Instead, he/she logs in with a security domain defined by the vSphere environment, and the authentication is done by the Single Sign-On Server. In vSphere 5.5, SSO was overhauled to fix several known issues with trusted multidomains often associated with enterprise corporations.

Advantages of vCenter Single Sign-On

vCenter Single Sign-On has the following advantages:

- As explained earlier, the authentication process that SSO follows is less complicated.

- It permits faster operations.

- It enables vSphere solutions to trust each other. Therefore, authentication is not required every time a linked product solution is accessed.

- It is an architecture which supports multi-instance and multi-site configurations. They provide single-solution authentication across the environment.

- It can work with multiple user repositories, which are known as **Identity Sources**. This means that the authentication can happen against multiple Microsoft **Active Directory Domain Services** (**ADDS**) environments.

Characteristics of vCenter Single Sign-On

Following are the characteristics of vCenter Single Sign-On:

- It supports open standards.

- It supports multiple user repositories. They include Microsoft AD DS and OpenLDAP.

- It enables the users to see all the vCenter Server instances they are eligible to access.

- There is no need to use vCenter Linked Mode for unified views of vCenter Server instances.

Managing inventory, hosts, VMs, and templates via vCenter

The vCenter Server inventory is a hierarchy of objects. This object hierarchy includes folders, which contain virtual machines and templates, and also clusters containing multiple ESXi hosts. Other objects that are visible in the inventory object tree are resource pools, data stores, and networks. The objects are grouped in a relevant way, so that together they provide a natural structure over which permissions are applied.

The topmost element of the vCenter Server Inventory hierarchy is known as **Root Object**, which is nothing more than the vCenter Server itself. It can't be removed from the entire inventory.

Data center objects

It is an important object in the vCenter Inventory Hierarchy. Objects are generally based on their geographical locations. Every data center object will have its own set of ESXi hosts, virtual machines, networks, and data stores.

In order to represent organizations or business units, companies may create multiple data center objects. Inventory objects interact within the data center but the interaction is very limited across different data centers.

Organizing the inventory objects

The items of the data center can be arranged in the form of folders. The folders are further fragmented into subfolders to organize the systems in a more immaculate way.

The benefit of arranging the objects in the form of folders and subfolders is that through this structure, suitable access can be given to administrators.

It should always be kept in mind that adding too many subfolders to a hierarchy makes its management difficult. So it should be designed with care. It is a common practice to create (sub) folders for particular applications and organization units (for example, company departments).

Navigating the vSphere Web Client

The inventory objects can be managed by vSphere Web Client. When the user is logged into the vCenter Server for the first time, using the vSphere Web Client, the home page is displayed. The home page contains a menu bar, a search box, and panels. This is the default layout. Navigation to the vSphere Web Client functions: inventories, monitoring, and administration can be done from the home page as it contains icons that redirect them to these functions.

If the user logs out of the vSphere Web Client, the view, which was visible when the client was closed, is saved. The next time the user logs in, the same view is visible to the user.

The vSphere Web Client contains a search field. This search field is present for all the views.

- **Hosts and clusters view**: The hosts and clusters view displays all the hosts and clusters information, and related virtual machines in the data center.
- **VMs and templates view**: The VMs and templates inventory view displays all virtual machines and templates objects in the data center.

- **Networking view**: The networking view displays all virtual machine port groups and distributed switches created inside the data center.

- **Storage view**: The storage inventory view displays all the details related to all the data stores in the data center. It displays all the storages, whether local storage or storages from SAN or NAS.

Adding the host to vCenter Server

Following are the steps to add the ESXi hosts to the vCenter Server:

1. To add the ESXi host to your vCenter, right-click the cluster or the data center Object and select **Add Host**.

2. The Add host wizard will start.

3. Specify fully qualified host name or IP address of the ESXi host.

4. Enter the hosts root username and password.

5. Specify lockdown mode settings.

Lockdown mode, if enabled, disables remote access for the root account after vCenter Server takes control of the host. This mode is used if we want that the host should be managed only by vCenter Server. Note that this makes managing the host harder if vCenter Server is unavailable.

vCenter Server licensing

In the VMware vSphere environment, the licensing is managed through vCenter Server. All licensing is encapsulated in 25-character license keys that can be managed and monitored from vCenter Server.

License information can be viewed by product, licensed key, or asset:

- **Product**: A license to use a vSphere software component or a particular feature

- **License Key**: The serial number that is related to a particular product

- **Asset**: The machine on which the product is installed

Backing up vCenter Server

Backup of vCenter Server depends on which deployment strategy was undertaken. If the vCenter Server is a physical system, then the method used will be different than if vCenter Server is deployed as an appliance.

The recommended practice is to take a full backup of your vCenter Server system. Keep in mind that VMware does not support installing third-party backup agents, so you will need to use a backup product that supports agentless VM backup. A very common practice is to use the VMware Data Protection Appliance or any other products that also use the vStorage API for Data Protection (VADP).

Before starting a conventional backup, the following services should be stopped:

- vCenter Server Service
- vCenter Inventory Service
- vCenter Single Sign-On Service
- VMware VCMSDS (active directory application mode database) service
- Database services

vCenter Server depends on its database, and the backup of the database should be taken according to the database solution which is used. For example, if Microsoft SQL server is used, then the backup should be done according to Microsoft SQL Server guidelines.

The SSL certificates and the `vpxd.cfg` files should also be backed up. For vCenter Server Appliance 5.5, VMware offers several useful articles describing the complete backup processes of the particular appliance components:

- Backing up and restoring the vCenter Server Appliance vPostgres database: `http://kb.vmware.com/kb/2034505`
- Backing up and restoring the vCenter Single Sign-On 5.5 configuration for the vCenter Server Appliance: `http://kb.vmware.com/kb/2063260`
- Backing up and restoring the vCenter Server Appliance Inventory Service database: `http://kb.vmware.com/kb/2062682`

Implementing an appropriate backup is an essential task, which should be planned and also tested carefully. Make sure to also test disaster recovery scenarios in productive setups. Losing the vCenter Server and having no valid backup might require a re-installation of vCenter Server.

Summary

In this chapter, we discussed that vCenter is the centralized management tool by VMware, and it is used to manage multiple ESXi hosts and virtual machines from a single centralized location. It can be accessed using the vSphere Client or the Web Client. In order to use the vCenter Server, we need to install the vCenter Server Appliance or install vCenter Server on a Microsoft Windows Server system. The vCenter Appliance enables the administrator the ability to configure the vCenter Server for use. Once configured properly, vCenter Server can be used to manage the server's inventory, ESXi hosts, virtual machines, and other infrastructure components. vCenter Server is also responsible for managing the licensing of the vSphere infrastructure.

In the next chapter, we will cover basic operations with a virtual machine, such as different methods of creation, thin and thick provisioning of a VM, installation of operating systems in VMs, and creating clones/templates.

3

Creating Virtual Machines

In the previous chapter, we discussed about vCenter Server and how it acts as the centralized management console for the vSphere environment. It is established that vCenter is used to manage multiple ESXi hosts and virtual machines from a centralized location. It is accessed using the vSphere legacy client or vSphere Web Client.

In this chapter, we will cover basic operations with a virtual machine, such as creation, provisioning, guest operating system installation, and creating clones/templates. This chapter will cover the following topics and act as a step by step guide to perform the listed operations with virtual machines:

- Overview of virtual machines
- Creating a virtual machine
- Creating a virtual machine using an OVF template
- Thick and Thin Provisioning of virtual disks
- Installing a guest operating system
- Creating templates and clones

Overview of virtual machines

Before we dive into operations that can be performed on virtual machines, let us first take an overview about virtual machines and the files that they are made up of. The generic definition of a virtual machine states that it is a mediation to the host CPU's hardware virtualization features. A virtual machine is a software implementation of a computer machine. Note that it is not emulation, as an emulator would also emulate the complete CPU, which is not applicable to vSphere. A virtual machine executes the processes in the same way a physical computer does. It provides a complete set of system platform on which an operating system and a set of applications can run.

However, as per VMware, a virtual Machine is a set of virtual hardware and features (in software format), in which a supported guest operating system and its applications can run. It is a set of discrete files. When a virtual machine is created, it creates with itself, a set of files which are used for specific purposes.

We will now discuss more about the set of particular files.

Virtual machine files

Whenever a virtual machine is created, a set of files is created during the process. Some of the files are created when the virtual machine is powered on, and some are created when a particular function is being called upon the machine. But each of these files has a significant role to play in the smooth operations/functioning of the virtual machine.

Following table shows the set of files created for a virtual machine named **VM** as an example:

File extension	File name	Description
`.vmx`	`VM.vmx`	Virtual machine configuration file
`.nvram`	`VM.nvram`	VM's virtual BIOS configuration and NVRAM state
`.vmdk`	`VM.vmdk`	VM's disk descriptor file
`-Flat.vmdk`	`VM-flat.vmdk`	VM's actual data (storage) file (OS/application, data)
`.vswp`	`VM.vswp`	VM's swap file (similar to Swap files in Linux)
`.vmsd`	`VM.vmsd`	VM's snapshot manager file
`.vmsn`	`VM.vmsn`	VM's snapshot state file
`-00000#.vmdk`	`VM-000001.vmdk`	VM's snapshot disk descriptor file
`-00000#-delta.vmdk`	`VM-000001-flat.vmdk`	Snapshot disk data file
`vmware.log`	`vmware.log`	Log file for every virtual machine; older logs are kept and renamed (`vmware.log.1`, `vmware.log.2,...`)
`.rdm`	`VM.rdm`	Raw device mapping file
`.vmss`	`VM.vmss`	Virtual machine state file

The following screenshot displays the virtual machine files for Windows 7:

Name	Size	Modified	Type	Path
Windows 7.vmdk	41,943,040 KB	5/18/15, 10:36...	Virtual Disk	[ESXi04_VMs] Windows 7/Windows 7.vmdk
Windows 7.vmx	2.8 KB	5/18/15, 10:39...	Virtual Machine	[ESXi04_VMs] Windows 7/Windows 7.vmx
Windows 7.vmx~	2.75 KB	5/18/15, 10:39...	File	[ESXi04_VMs] Windows 7/Windows 7.vmx~
Windows 7.vmx.lck	0 KB	5/18/15, 10:39...	File	[ESXi04_VMs] Windows 7/Windows 7.vmx.lck
vmx-Windows 7-3816208481-1.vswp	194,560 KB	5/18/15, 10:39...	File	[ESXi04_VMs] Windows 7/vmx-Windows 7-3816208481-1.vswp
Windows 7.nvram	8.48 KB	5/18/15, 10:39...	Non-volatile Memory File	[ESXi04_VMs] Windows 7/Windows 7.nvram
Windows 7-e376b861.vswp	2,097,152 KB	5/18/15, 10:39...	File	[ESXi04_VMs] Windows 7/Windows 7-e376b861.vswp
vmware.log	117.21 KB	5/18/15, 10:39...	VM Log File	[ESXi04_VMs] Windows 7/vmware.log
Windows 7.vmsd	0 KB	5/18/15, 10:36...	File	[ESXi04_VMs] Windows 7/Windows 7.vmsd

Virtual hardware versions

A virtual machine is created on the basis of a set of virtual hardware and features called virtual hardware (often also called vHW or VMHW version). During deployment of a virtual machine using the custom wizard, it is possible to specify a particular vHW version. Depending on the virtual machine's guest operating system, it might be necessary to choose a specific version.

The following table shows major differences between the last three virtual hardware versions:

	vSphere 5.1	vSphere 5.5	vSphere 6.0
Maximum vHW	Version 9	Version 10	Version 11
Virtual CPUs	64		128
Virtual RAM	1 TB		4 TB
vDisk size	2 TB	62 TB	
SCSI adapters / targets	4 / 60		
SATA adapters / targets	Not supported	4 / 30	
Nvidia vGPU	Not supported		Yes
Parallel / Serial ports	3 / 4		3 / 32

Some guest operating systems require a newer virtual hardware version. VMware offers a very comprehensive list of supported guest operating systems at

```
http://www.vmware.com/resources/compatibility/search.
php?deviceCategory=software
```

The oldest virtual hardware version, supported on all vSphere releases mentioned above, is vHW 4 (ESXi 3.x). It is possible to upgrade a virtual machine's vHW version. Note that this process cannot be undone. Make sure to create a backup of the virtual machine and check in advance whether the guest operating system is supported on the new vHW release. Once updated, a downgrade is not possible. The vSphere legacy client is not supported to add new features that came with vHW release 9 or higher (for example, USB 3.0 xHCI controllers), but it is possible to edit previously supported features. It is a common practice to use vSphere Web Client for virtual machines with vHW version 9 or higher.

Creating a virtual machine

An administrator can create a virtual machine using many different methods. In this chapter, we will cover how an administrator can create virtual machines manually. The two methods which we will discuss are:

- Creating a virtual machine using the **New Virtual Machine Wizard**
- Importing a virtual appliance

Creating a new virtual machine using the wizard

An Administrator can open **New Virtual Machine Wizard** using the vSphere legacy client or vSphere Web Client, to create a virtual machine. Creating a virtual machine using the wizard is very simple; once the wizard is open, you just have to feed the right information to it and the virtual machine is created.

The following steps need to be performed in each scenario:

- **Creating through a vSphere legacy client**: Right-click the ESXi host in the inventory and select **New Virtual Machine**
- **Creating through vSphere Web Client**: From the data center or host in the inventory, right-click the **Action** menu and click **New Virtual Machine**

The following screenshot shows the menu item in vSphere Web Client for creating new virtual machines.

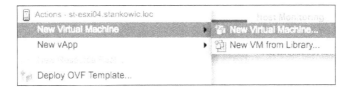

Once the **New Virtual Machine Wizard** starts, the administrator can choose between a **Typical** and **Custom** configuration to create a virtual machine. However, you do not get this option if you are using vSphere Web Client to create the new virtual machine by using the wizard.

Regardless of the location from where the administrator is trying to create the virtual machine, the following information has to be provided:

- The virtual machine's name
- The data store on which to store the virtual machine files
- The guest operating system which will be installed
- The number of NICs and the virtual network to connect to
- Virtual disk provisioning type

If the user selects to create the virtual machine with the Custom configuration, the following additional information is required:

- Virtual machine hardware version (version 10 being the latest)
- Number of CPUs and cores per CPU
- Size of the memory
- SCSI controller type
- Whether to create a disk, use an existing disk, create a RDM, or use no disk
- Whether to store the **virtual machine disk** (**vmdk**) with the virtual machine files or on a separate data store.
- Mode-Independent (persistent disk or nonpersistent disk)

The persistent disk commits the changes immediately and permanently when any data is written to it. The nonpersistent disk discards the changes when a virtual machine is powered off.

Regardless of the configuration type selected, the administrator can attach an ISO image to the virtual CD/DVD drive after the virtual machine is created.

Importing an OVF file

An administrator can deploy virtual appliances using a **Open Virtualization Format** (**OVF**) template. A virtual appliance is basically one or multiple preconfigured virtual machines. It includes a preinstalled guest operating system and other software. The administrator doesn't need to install any operating system on the new virtual machine as it is already installed and is ready to use. A virtual appliance is designed for a specific purpose, for example, to provide a secure web browser, a firewall, backup server, or recovery utility. In the previous chapter, we learned that vCenter Server Appliance is also deployed using an OVF template.

A virtual appliance can be added, removed, or imported to vCenter Server or an ESXi host inventory. Virtual appliances are deployed as an OVF template. OVF is a platform-independent, efficient, extensible, and open platform for distributing virtual appliances. OVF templates are in compressed format and are easy to download. Virtual appliances can also be imported from VMware Virtual Appliance Marketplace at

```
https://solutionexchange.vmware.com/store/category_groups/virtual-
appliances.
```

The vSphere Web Client validates an OVF file before importing it and ensures that it is compatible with the destination server on which it will be imported. If the appliance is not compatible with the server, then it cannot be imported.

To import a virtual appliance, perform the following steps:

1. Select the host or cluster in the inventory, select the **Actions** menu, and click **Deploy OVF Template...**.
2. Point to the OVF file from where the virtual appliance will be imported.
3. Enter a VM name and select the data store the template will be deployed on.
4. Some OVF templates require additional information like network settings. If applicable, enter them.
5. Review and acknowledge the configuration.

The following screenshots shows the menu item in vSphere Web Client for deploying OVF templates:

Thick and thin provisioning of virtual disks

Virtual disk provisioning is the process of managing storage space by allocating storage space on "as and when needed" basis. This simplifies storage administration by meeting capacity allocation on request. When creating a virtual disk for the virtual machine, there are three disk types available:

- **Thick Provision Lazy-Zeroed**: When this option is selected, a virtual disk is created in a default thick format. If we create a 20 GB disk with this type, then 20 GB space is reserved for the virtual disk. However, the data on the physical device is not erased during the creation process; instead it is zeroed (erased) out on demand later during write operations on unused blocks inside the virtual machine.

- **Thick Provision Eager-Zeroed**: When this option is selected, the complete space is allocated to the virtual disk during the time of creation. In contrast to Lazy-Zeroed, the data remaining on the physical device is zeroed out during the creation process. Thick Provisioned Eager zeroed supports clustering features like fault tolerance and offers the best I/O performance.

- **Thin Provision**: This format is used to save storage space. An administrator can provision as much datastore space as the disk would require; however, the thin disk starts small at first and uses as much disk as it requires for its operations, and rest of the disk space is unconsumed. Note that over-allocating datastores requires a higher level of management and alerting, to ensure not filling up a LUN. If a datastore containing a virtual machine's virtual disk has no remaining storage capacity, the virtual machine will be paused to avoid data corruption. Thin Provision is often used along with **Virtual Desktop Infrastructure** (**VDI**) setups and Linked Clones, as the high amount of virtual machines share virtual disk blocks to reduce storage needs.

Installing a guest operating system

Installing a guest operating system is the same as installing the operating system in a physical machine. To install a guest operating system, perform the following steps:

1. Connect to the virtual machine using the console tab.

2. The administrator can attach the ISO image on to the virtual CD/DVD drive, or directly connect to the physical ESXi host's CD/DVD drive. It is also possible to pass through the CD/DVD drive of the computer accessing the virtual machine's console.

3. Install the operating system.

Customizing the guest operating system

Whether cloning a virtual machine or deploying a virtual machine from a template, an administrator can customize its guest operating system to change certain properties, such as the following:

- Hostname
- License information
- Network settings

Customizing the guest operating system can help prevent the software and network conflict, which occurs when the virtual machines with identical configuration are created. The conflicts can be due to similar hostnames or IP addresses.

Administrator can create the customization specifications in Customization Specification Manager. These customization specifications are stored in the vCenter Server database. During cloning or deploying, the administrator can select the specification to be applied to the virtual machine.

Implementing customization specifications is an advanced topic that depends on the guest operating system chosen by the user. VMware offers a great documentation about this feature, available at `https://pubs.vmware.com/vsphere-51/index.jsp?topic=%2Fcom.vmware.vsphere.vm_admin.doc%2FGUID-EB5F090E-723C-4470-B640-50B35D1EC016.html`

VMware Tools

VMware tools VMware Tools is a set of special drivers and also utilities that enhance the performance of the operating system running inside the virtual machine.

Installing VMware Tools is not mandatory, but it is the best practice to install them in all the virtual machines. VMware Tools, when installed, provide the following benefits:

- Device drivers such as SVGA, network card, and Ballooning drivers for memory management and improved mouse performance
- Virtual machine heartbeat
- Time synchronization of the guest operating system with ESXi server
- Ability to shut down the virtual machine
- Additional performance monitoring options

The VMware Tools installation process differs per guest operating system. For example, Windows systems will show a graphical installation wizard, while Linux systems will have a command line-interface setup utility, based on the Perl language.

To install VMware Tools, select the virtual machine from the inventory and right-click **All vCenter Tasks | Guest Operating System | Install/Upgrade VMware Tools**. For the vSphere legacy client, the user has to select **Inventory | Virtual Machine | Guest | Install/Upgrade VMware Tools**.

Creating templates and clones

A template is a master copy of a virtual machine. It is used to create and provision multiple other virtual machines of same type, including the same guest operating system and its configuration.

A template generally includes the following:

- A guest operating system
- A set of applications
- Virtual hardware configuration

Creating a template makes the provisioning of multiple virtual machines faster and easier. It is very easy to deploy virtual machines from a template, and it saves a lot of time which was otherwise used in installing the guest operating system and applications.

A template can be created in many ways:

- **Clone a Virtual Machine to Template**: The virtual machine's power status doesn't affect this process; it can be powered on or off. In this case, we will continue to have the original virtual machine, and a new template of the same virtual machine will also be created.

- **Convert a Virtual Machine to a Template**: The virtual machine should be powered off. In this case, the original virtual machine is no longer present and it is converted to a template.

- **Clone a Template**: In this, we duplicate an already created template. As a template is already in powered-off state, the cloned template will also be in the same state.

Deploying a virtual machine from a template

The following steps are required to deploy a virtual machine from a template:

1. Select the template in the **VMs and Templates** view.
2. Right-click the template and select **Deploy VM from this Template**.

The deploy template wizard will start and prompt for information related to virtual machine deployment.

The following screenshots shows the menu item in vSphere Web Client for deploying virtual machines from templates:

Cloning a virtual machine

Cloning a virtual machine is an alternative to deploying a virtual machine from a template. Cloning a virtual machine creates an exact copy of the virtual machine with same set of operating system, applications, and virtual hardware.

The virtual machine power state doesn't matter, that is, a virtual machine can be in powered on or powered off state.

To clone a virtual machine, right-click **Virtual machine** in the inventory and select **Clone to Virtual Machine...** option. Refer to the following image:

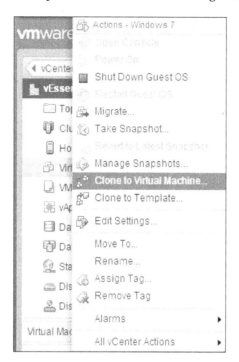

Summary

In this chapter, we covered basic operations with a virtual machine, such as creation, provisioning, installation in VMs, creating clones/templates, and so on. We read and understood that there are multiple ways of creating a virtual machine and one can pick any of these as per his requirements. We also learned about various configuration parameters for a virtual machine, and how to provision a virtual machine. In addition, we learned about installing operating system on virtual machines and configuring it. The chapter also covered a step by step process of creating templates and clones.

In next chapter, we will cover network management in a VMware virtual infrastructure. We will cover and understand various virtual network components, virtual switches, and virtual ports. The following screenshots shows the menu item in vSphere Web Client for deploying virtual machines from templates.

4
Managing Virtual Network

In the previous chapter, we covered basic operations with a virtual machine such as creation, provisioning, guest operating system installation, creating clones/templates, and so on. We learned about disk provisioning, and cloning of virtual machines and templates.

In this chapter, we will cover network management in a VMware virtual infrastructure. We will cover and understand various virtual network components, virtual switches, and virtual ports. After this chapter, you will understand essential virtual networking concepts such as VLANs. You will also be able to create and configure network security policies, NIC teaming and load-balancing.

Following is the list of topics we will go through in this chapter:

- Basic network operations using vSphere
- Understanding virtual network components and their implementation
- Virtual switch types, components, and ports
- Creating VLANs
- Network and security policies
- Load-balancing with vSphere

vSphere networking allows virtual machines to communicate with one another, and with other physical machines. It helps in the management of ESXi hosts, vMotion migration, Fault Tolerance, IP based storage, and so on. As an administrator, one should be aware of all the features and functionalities which are offered by VMware. Network design and configuration is an essential task that should be planned carefully. Keep in mind that erroneous configurations might negatively affect the environment.

Virtual network

Virtual network provides the networking for virtual machines and ESXi hosts. Like we have physical switches in our physical network, in virtual network the fundamental component is a virtual switch.

An overview of virtual switches

A virtual switch is a software-based switch built inside the ESXi kernel (VMkernel), which is used to provide networking for the virtual environment. The traffic which flows from/to virtual machines is passed through one of the virtual switches present in VMkernel. So the virtual switch provides the connection for virtual machines to communicate with each other, whether they are running on the same host or on different hosts.

A virtual switch allows management of ESXi hosts, migration of virtual machines, and access to IP based storage. A virtual switch works at Layer 2 of the OSI model. We cannot have more than one virtual switch connected to the same physical NIC, but we can have more than one physical NIC connected to the same virtual switch. We can combine the bandwidth of multiple physical NICs and load balance the traffic among them, and load balance the traffic among them. To enhance availability, we can also configure multiple NICs in fail-over mode to avoid network failures.

Basic network operations using vSphere

VMware vSphere offers a wide array of features and flexibility when networking is in consideration. To establish effective communication among ESXi hosts and storage, proper network configurations are essential. We will be discussing few basic network operations which are critical in nature and are required for basic minimum activities in every virtual environment.

Assigning an IP address to an ESXi host

Every ESXi host must have an IP address assigned to it; the recommendation is to use static IP addresses. ESXi IP addresses can be assigned using **Direct Console User Interface (DCUI)**.

To log into DCUI, connect to the console of the ESXi host. This can be done by plugging a monitor to the physical server, or by using a remote access utility such as HP iLO or DELL iDRAC. Press the *F2* key and enter the user credentials for logging into the server, and then go to the **Configure Management Network** tab, as shown in the following screenshot:

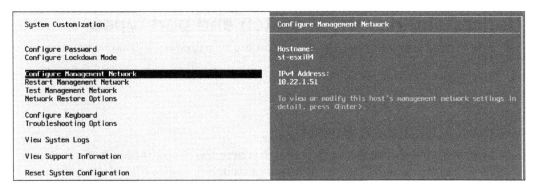

Once on **Configure Management Network**, select **IP Configuration** and enter the desired IP settings. Refer to the following screenshot:

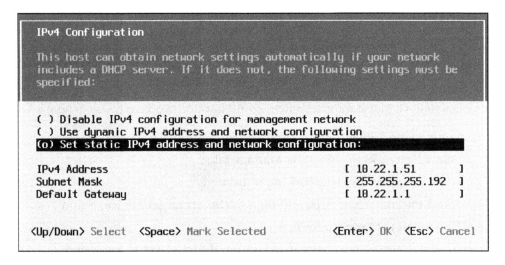

Depending on your server's hardware configuration, you might also need to pick one or multiple, specific NICs. This can be done by accessing the **Network Adapters** pane and selecting all the needed NICs.

Creating vSwitches and virtual ports

Virtual switches and ports are the key components in the networking of any virtual infrastructure. Creating virtual switches and ports is explained step by step in the next sections of this chapter.

Understanding virtual switch and port types

VMware virtual network provides the following two types of virtual switches:

- vNetwork Standard Virtual Switch
- vNetwork Distributed Virtual Switch

vNetwork Standard Switch

A standard virtual switch is a virtual switch where the configuration is done at host level. It works like a layer 2 physical Ethernet switch. It is also often called vSwitch or vSS. You can have up to 4088 ports per standard switch but the total number of virtual switch ports on a single ESXi host can only be 4096. The default number of virtual ports can be 120 per standard switch on vSphere 5.5 and 6.0.

To view a host's standard virtual switch configuration, you can click on the networking link on the host's manage tab, when connecting through vSphere Web Client. By default, when we install ESXi, a standard virtual switch (vSwitch0) is created. Also, one virtual machine port group by the name **VM Network** and VM kernel port named **Management Network** are created as well.

To create a new virtual standard switch, administrator needs to ESXi's manage tab.

1. Login using vSphere Web Client.
2. Select **Networking** under the **Manage** tab.
3. Click the **Add Host Networking** button.
4. Select the connection type and then the **Select target device** option.
5. Choose **New Standard Switch**.
6. Add all physical network cards that should be added to the switch.
7. Review your changes.

The following screenshot shows the Add Networking wizard while creating a new standard switch:

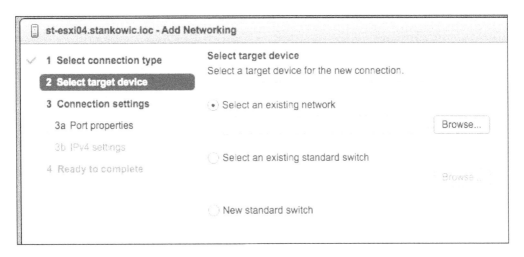

vNetwork Distributed Virtual Switch

A vNetwork Distributed Virtual Switch provides more functionality than a vSwitch including advanced features such as Link Layer Discovery Protocol (LLDP) and port mirroring. It functions as a single virtual switch across all associated ESXi hosts. This switch type is also called **dvSwitch** or **vDS**. Distributed virtual switch is created through vCenter Server, which owns its configuration. For vSphere 5.5 and 6.0, we can create up to 128 distributed switches per vCenter Server, and 16 distributed switches per ESXi host. Although a distributed switch is created at vCenter Server, some configurations are still specific to ESXi hosts, such as the uplinks (physical links) that are allocated to the distributed switch.

To create a virtual distributed switch, click on the **Networking** pane right-click on the data center object. In the pop-up menu, click the **New Distributed Switch** option as illustrated in the following screenshot:

1. Login using vSphere Web Client.
2. In **Navigator**, select the **Networking** pane.
3. Make sure you have created a virtual data center, as a distributed virtual switch requires this. If not, click **Create Data center** first. Define a name and acknowledge the creation.
4. Select **Create a distributed switch**.

5. Enter a switch name.

6. Choose the distributed switch version. Make sure to select a version that all your ESXi hosts support. If you're running a cluster with various versions (for example, 5.5 and 6.0), you need to select the highest version that all nodes support – in this case, 5.5.

7. Define the number of uplinks and a port group name. If you don't want to create a port group during the switch creation, unselect **Create a default port group**.

8. Check and acknowledge your settings.

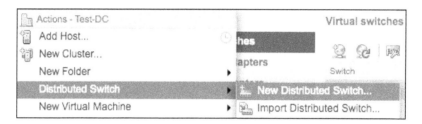

After creating the distributed virtual switch, it is necessary to connect the particular ESXi hosts to it. To do so, perform the following steps:

1. Select the distributed virtual switch, right-click **Add and Manage hosts**, and select **Add hosts** in the wizard.

2. Click **New hosts** and select all hosts you want to connect to the switch.

3. Select **Manage physical adapters** and **Manage VMkernel adapters** to migrate physical NIC and VMkernel ports into the distributed virtual switch. If you also want to migrate VM networks, you need to check **Migrate virtual machine networking**.

4. Select all physical adapters you want to migrate and select an uplink port for every NIC.

5. Choose a port group for management traffic by clicking **Assign port group** per ESXi host. Note that you might need to create a distributed virtual port group first.

6. If you're using iSCSI for virtual machine storage, a summary will be displayed. If a connection lost is indispensable, you will be notified. In this case, it might be safer to shutdown all affected virtual machines first.

7. Select port groups for running the virtual machines.

8. Review and confirm your settings.

Benefits of distributed over standard

Distributed switches offer a wide array of benefits over standard switches. A few of them are listed as follows:

- Distributed switches have a centralized networking configuration. Instead of doing the configuration on every host, we can do it at the vCenter Server level and implement across all the ESXi hosts.

- Private VLAN configuration is only supported by distributed virtual switches. Although VLAN tagging and untagging is supported by standard virtual switches, private VLAN is not supported.

- Distributed virtual switches make vMotion easier, as all the ESXi hosts share the same virtual networking.

- Certain advanced features like port mirroring and blocking, NetFlow, and network resource pools are only supported by distributed virtual switches.

On the other hand, there are also disadvantages that new users should be aware of. These are listed next:

- Distributed virtual switches require the most expensive Enterprise Plus vSphere license

- Managing distributed virtual switches is way more complex and might confuse new users

- Losing the vCenter Server results in being unable to manage the network

Virtual switch ports

A virtual switch provides the following two types of ports:

- **Virtual machine ports**: Every virtual machine connects to a particular virtual port on a virtual switch. The collection of virtual machine ports is generally referred as a virtual machine port group.

- **VMkernel Port**: A VMkernel port is used for services such as management of ESXi hosts, vMotion, Fault Tolerance, and for accessing IP-based storage.

It is a very common approach to create dedicated VMkernel ports for management traffic, vMotion, and IP-based storage to ensure that particular essential services don't interfere with each other. Especially vMotion and fault tolerance require a dedicated, high-performance network; the recommendation for the most recent vSphere release is to use 10 Gbps components. It is a common practice to separate virtual machine traffic from management traffic.

To add a new port, the administrator needs to navigate to ESXi's manage tab. Select **Networking** under the **Manage** tab and click the **Add Host Networking** button. Now select the appropriate port type from the **Add Networking** dialog box, as displayed in the following screenshot:

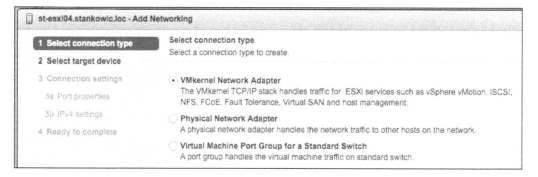

Whenever an IP address is assigned to an ESXi host, it is assigned to the VMkernel port instead of the NIC port, as compared to the physical environment.

Design ideas

When planning the network design of a vSphere infrastructure, the administrator has to take care of multiple requirements, including:

- Load balancing
- Fault tolerance
- Scale-out planning
- Integration in pre-existing network infrastructure

New users might have problems with creating a reasonable network design. Having some practical examples can help newcomers with designing their own infrastructure. Consider the following two examples:

Blade server-based approach

I have been using this design on several blade server-based designs. The blade servers that I used offered two NICs with two ports each. The requirement was to implement a fault-tolerance management/cluster and virtual machine network.

The following figure demonstrates the assigment of physical NICs on the blade servers:

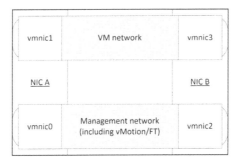

Let's summarize the previous drawing:

- The blade server offers two NICs: NIC A and NIC B, both having 2 ports
- Virtual switches are created using one port of both NICs to ensure having at least one network uplink if one NIC is faulty
- Dedicated virtual switches are created for management/cluster network (including vMotion and fault tolerance), and virtual machine traffic

Rack server-based approach

Rack server-based design mostly offers more physical network ports than the Blade server-based approach. Again, the requirement was to implement a fault tolerant management and virtual machine network like in the example before. In addition to that a dedicated network for an iSCSI-based SAN was created. As we have more ports than on the Blade server approach, there are spare ports for future use.

The following figure explains the assigment of physical NICs to logical networks:

vmnic3	unused	vmnic7	unused	vmnic11
vmnic2	VM network	vmnic6	VM network	vmnic10
NIC A		NIC B		NIC C
vmnic1	iSCSI storage	vmnic5	iSCSI storage	vmnic9
vmnic0	Management network	vmnic4	(including vMotion/FT)	vmnic8

Let's have a deeper look at this more complex setup:

- The rack server offers three NICs (NIC A, B, and C) with 4 ports each
- Virtual switches are created using one port of all three NICs to ensure having network connectivity even if one or multiple NICs are faulty
- Dedicated virtual switches are created for management/cluster network, iSCSI storage, and VM traffic
- There are three unused ports which could be assigned later to enable more network throughput on demand

Additional ideas for optimizing fault tolerance network designs

Making a server's network configuration more robust and fault-tolerance by using multiple NICs is the first step for a highly available vSphere infrastructure. On the other hand, it is also necessary to do the same for other infrastructure components, including network infrastructure such as switches. A very often used approach to ensure this, is to use multiple switches and connect the particular NIC ports to another switch.

The following figure demonstrates how to assign the particular NICs to switches to make the network design more robust.

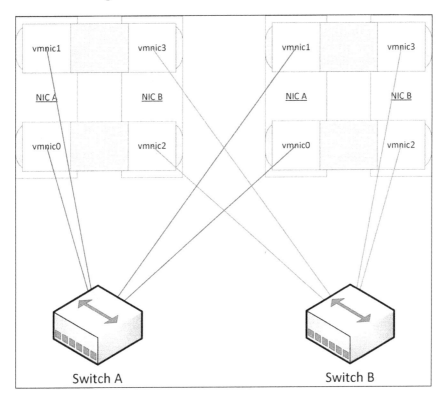

If one of the switches being used crashes, the particular NICs still have another uplink on the other switch. This means doubled costs for the two switches, but it also results in higher availability and expunging the switch as single point of failure. When using fibre-channel storage systems, an approach would be to do the same for storage switches.

Designing a reliable and highly available vSphere infrastructure design is a complex task, which should be planned and tested together with all infrastructure responsibles. As there is no generic answer to how to implement a reliable infrastructure setup, try to answer the following questions for your company's business:

- What does availability mean to us?
- How important are the workloads we're running?
- What time frame is sufficient for us to fix faulty infrastructure components?
- What does our budget look like?

Connecting a virtual machine to a port group

Virtual machines are connected to virtual switches using a port group. To connect a virtual machine to a port group on a distributed or standard switch, the following steps need to be performed:

1. Login using vSphere Web Client.
2. Right click the virtual machine and go to **Edit Settings.**
3. Click **Network adapter** in the **Virtual Hardware** pane.
4. From the drop-down menu, choose the desired port group.

The following screenshot shows the Edit Settings (SCREEN TEXT style) wizard for a particular VM:

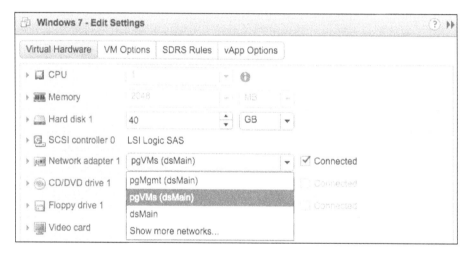

An overview of VLANs

VLANs are used to provide a logical isolation between different traffic types or network areas. In other words, they are used to provide logical partition to a single broadcast domain. What it means is that a single layer 2 network can be divided or partitioned into multiple distinct broadcast domains. VLANs are used to mutually isolate the traffic inside a single network by using VLAN IDs. VLAN configuration is either done at the switch level or at the router level. To have unique network connectivity, it is important to ensure that VLANs are carried to all participating switches. To sum it up, you need to keep VLAN configuration the same on all switches.

A trunk port is a port on a network switch which is configured to send and receive packets on more than one VLAN. VLANs offer a wide array of benefits over the standard network architecture. A few of the major change maker key benefits are:

- Network scalability
- Network security
- Network management
- Creation of logically grouped networks

ESXi supports 802.1Q VLAN tagging. In ESXi, VLANs are configured at port group level; the VLAN ID is provided to a port group on a distributed virtual switch. The VMkernel takes care of all the tagging and untagging activities as the packets pass through the virtual switch.

The switch port on the physical switch to which ESXi's physical NIC is connected must be configured as a static trunk port. Packets from the virtual machine are tagged as they exit the virtual switch and are untagged as they return to the virtual machines. VMware claims that the effect on the performance is minimal.

Creating VLANs

VLAN IDs are associated with port groups on the distributed virtual switch. VLANs in virtual environment are not manually created; they are only assigned VLAN IDs and are linked to the desired port groups.

To link VLAN ID to a port group, go to the **Edit Settings** page of the port group and under the **Properties** pane, select **VLAN ID**.

The following screenshot demonstrates how to configure a VLAN using VMware vSphere Web Client:

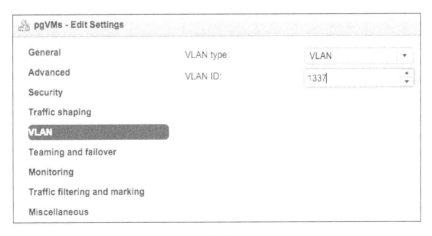

To assign a VLAN ID to a VMkernel port, go to **Edit Settings** of the VMkernel port and under the **Properties** pane, select **VLAN ID**.

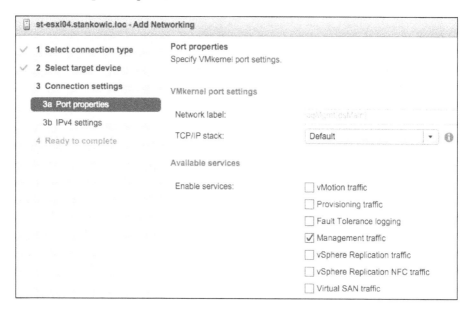

Network security policies

In standard virtual switches, three types of policies can be configured to implement security and to maximize the performance of the infrastructure. The implementation and usage may vary from architecture to architecture in different VMware environments. The three policies to optimize the infrastructure are:

- Security
- Traffic Shaping
- NIC teaming

Policies can be defined either at the standard virtual switch level, or at the port or port group level. The policies applied at the port group level over ride the policies (or take precedence over the policies) applied at the virtual switch level. Hence, it is advisable to implement all major and critical policies at the port group level.

Security policy

A VMware vSphere security policy consists of three policy exceptions, which are described as follows. These exceptions can be enabled/disabled as per requirements.

- **Promiscous mode**: Promiscous mode, when set to accept, passes all the traffic to all the ports, which flows through that particular virtual switch or the particular port group. It enables a vNIC on a virtual machine to receive a copy of all the packets on the same vSwitch or port group. By default, it is set to reject. If we're using some kind of packet sniffer as an application inside a virtual machine we need to accept promiscous mode. A common usecase for this is running networking monitoring software inside virtual machines.

- **MAC address changes**: A MAC address is a hexadecimal number which is assigned to all the networking components. In VMware environment, each virtual machine vNIC is assigned a MAC address when a virtual machine is powered on. This security feature allows an operating system, running inside the virtual machine, to change its MAC address. So, if the user is using a particular virtual machine and changes the MAC address from inside the operating system, and the policy is set to accept, the virtual switch will not drop the packets. However, if its set to reject, the packets will be dropped.

- **Forged transmits**: Forged transmit is similar to MAC address changes, except that the forged transmits deal with the traffic that. originates from a virtual machine rather than which is received by the virtual machines. So basically, if a user changes a MAC address from inside the guest operating system and the policy is set to reject, the packets sent out will be dropped. While the MAC address changes policy applies to incoming traffic, this policy addresses the outgoing traffic. Altering this policy might be necessary for some network scanner utilities.

To implement security policies for an ESXi host's virtual standard switch, following are the steps:

1. Click on the ESXi host in the inventory, click **Manage,** and choose **Networking**.
2. Under **Virtual Switches**, select **Edit Settings**.
3. Select the **Security** option and set parameters as desired.

To implement security policies for distributed virtual switches, follow the steps listed next:

1. Select the **Networking** pane in the overview.
2. Select a distributed virtual port group from the inventory.
3. Right-click **Edit Settings** and open the **Security** pane.
4. Select parameters as desired.

Traffic shaping

Traffic shaping is a feature which allows the administrator to control the amount of bandwidth that a virtual switch can transmit. The traffic shaping policy in a standard virtual switch is only for the outbound traffic. If the administrator wants to configure inbound traffic shaping also, then distributed virtual switches need to be used. There are three configuration parameters in traffic shaping. These are:

- **Average Bandwidth**: It refers to the guaranteed amount of bandwidth that we want to set for data transmission

- **Peak Bandwidth**: This is the maximum amount of bandwidth that a virtual switch can have to transmit data

- **Burst Size**: It is the specified number of bytes, each time a virtual switch bursts above the average bandwidth which was set

Average bandwidth and Peak bandwidth are specified in kilobits per second, while burst size is in kilobytes.

To implement the Traffic Shaping policy, following steps need to be followed:

1. Click on the ESXi host in the inventory, click **Manage,** and choose **Networking**.

2. Under **Virtual Switches**, select **Edit Settings**.

3. Select **Traffic Shaping** and set parameters as desired.

NIC teaming

NIC teaming policy enables the administrator to control the traffic flow and distribution between network adapters. It allows rerouting the traffic in case of an adapter failure or overload. NIC teaming policy combines load balancing and fail over features to provide better control over data passing over the network. By default, NIC teaming is implemented at the switch level for the entire standard switch. However, just like security policies, they can also be over ridden by any policies or exceptions that an administrator implements at port group level. Any policy changes made at the port group level get precedence over the default policy at the switch level.

NIC teaming policies are customizable and can be modified by following the steps mentioned next for a standard virtual switch:

1. Click on the ESXi host in the inventory, click **Manage,** and choose **Networking**.

2. Under **Virtual Switches**, select **Edit Settings**.

3. Select the **Teaming and Failover** option and set parameters as desired.

To implement NIC teaming on port group level, under **Virtual Switches**, select the desired port group and go to **Edit Settings**.

Load Balancing with vSphere

Load Balancing is the technique used to distribute network traffic across multiple network adapters, in order to divide the load on multiple network interface cards. There are four load balancing policies. These are:

- **Route based on originating Virtual Port ID**: In this method, the physical NIC is determined according to the virtual port ID to which the virtual machine is connected. It depends on the power on cycle of the virtual machines present on the host and connected to the same virtual switch or port group. In this method, the load is distributed evenly, which makes it one of the most used load balancing techniques in VMware environment.

- **Route based on source MAC hash**: In this load balancing method, the physical NIC is determined according to the MAC address of the virtual machine vNIC. This technique has a very low overhead, but might not be able to spread load evenly across physical NICs.

- **Route based on IP Hash**: In this method, the physical NIC is determined on the basis of the source and the destination's IP address. This technique has high CPU overhead but the load balancing is better across NICs. This method also requires that the switch ports are configured as EtherChannel; this requires features such as aggregation bonding, trunking, or port-channeling on the switch.

- **Explicit failover**: In Explicit failover, the most active physical NIC is used. It is not technically load balancing; the physical NIC, which is at the highest order of uplink from the list of all active physical NICs, will be used to transmit data.

Summary

In this chapter, we understood the core components of networking in a virtual infrastructure. To sum it up, we are now able to choose between vNetwork standard and distributed virtual switches to connect virtual machine traffic and management networks to our physical network infrastructure. While distributed virtual switches offer the most advanced networking functionality, we can also address most of the network requirements with virtual standard switches as well. vNetwork Standard switches are defined on every ESXi host in our environment if we want to lower the management effort, we can go for distributed virtual switches which are centrally defined and configured in vCenter Server.

Planning and designing a virtual network infrastructure is mandatory. To make our setup reliable, we can choose ports of multiple multiport NICs as uplinks for virtual switches. Another approach to optimize availability is to use multiple networking and for storage components to be more fault tolerant.

In the next chapter, we will have a look at VMware NSX, which enables us to improve flexibility and manageability of virtual networks even more. NSX is a quite new product and enables enhanced virtualization capabilities to include network infrastructure.

5

Network Virtualization with VMware NSX

In the previous chapter, we covered basic network operations under the VMkernel built network virtualization. We covered and understood the various virtual network components and their implementation, and also how to create VLANs. Security policies being one of the major crucial aspects of network management, was also covered, along with load balancing.

By the end of this chapter, you will be able to understand the features and use cases for VMware NSX. NSX is the latest offering from VMware and is very new to the market. However, it is an incredibly powerful tool to configure and manage virtual networks. We will begin with understanding NSX and what it does, review the steps involved in its installation, and make our way through access layer deployment in a data center. We will also find out how routing and switching works in NSX, and how can a firewall be implemented on a network managed by NSX. Anyway, network virtualization is a very complex topic that can only be touched in this chapter.

Following is the list of topics we will cover:

- NSX components
- Deploying NSX Manager
- Data center access layer deployment
- Logical routing, switching
- Firewall management and load-balancing

VMware NSX is a network virtualization platform, which delivers operational network functions from software. It recreates all network layers above the physical layer, that is, from layer 2 to 7. This allows configuring and creating network topologies for a virtual network. Being a fully powered networking solution, it also offers enhanced features for implementing network security, and allows full customization and flexibility to implement inbuilt and third party security and firewalls. NSX addresses the software-defined networking (SDN) philosophy and helps automate infrastructure delivery and maintenance tasks in modern virtual infrastructure setups.

In the last chapter, we discussed that a virtual network is made up of virtual network components such as virtual switches, routers, and so on. Similarly, NSX also comprises of logic based virtual components such as switches, routers, firewalls, load balancers, VPN gateways, and many more. NSX offers way more advanced options in network topology design and a lot more features than contemporary networking solutions in vSphere, hence making it a dedicated and a very strong network virtualization tool.

With the use of NSX in a data center, there comes a series of benefits in terms of computing, performance, efficiency, and agility of the data center. NSX can be configured using vCenter Web Client, command line interface, or the REST API.

NSX exists in the following two variants:

- VMware NSX for vSphere (NSX-v)
- VMware NSX for Multi-Hypervisor (NSX-MH)

NSX for vSphere (NSX-v) is specialized for vSphere infrastructure setups and offers the most advanced vSphere integration. NSX-v is only supported in ESXi-only hypervisor setups. On the other hand, VMware NSX for Multi-Hypervisors is open to integrate multiple hypervisors, such as KVM and Xen, and cloud architectures including CloudStack and OpenStack.

Let's summarize the major differences between the variants, through the following table:

	NSX-v	NSX-MH
Hypervisor support	ESXi only	ESXi, KVM, Xen
Management tools	NSX Manager	CloudStack, OpenStack
Virtual switches	vNetwork Distributed Switch (vDS)	Open vSwitch (OVS)

	NSX-v	**NSX-MH**
Encapsulation	Virtual Extensible LAN (VXLAN)	VXLAN, Stateless Transport Tunneling (STT), Generic Routing Encapsulation Protocol (GRE)
VPN gateway	Yes	No
Load balancer	Yes	No
Service Composer	Yes	No
L2 switching (logical, physical)	Yes	
QoS	Yes	
L3 distributed switching	Yes	
Dynamic routing	Yes	No
Dynamic firewall	Stateful distributed, layer 2 to 4	Stateless distributed, layer 2 to 4

NSX is a very powerful add-on to the vSphere environment and offers a wide array of features when implemented properly. A few key features of NSX are:

- **Logical Switching**: NSX reproduces the whole layer 2 and layer 3 switching functions as per the vSphere virtual environment. It does this by decoupling the switching functionalities for the physical hardware installed on the server.

- **NSX Gateway**: NSX gateway service offers layer 2 gateway mechanisms for stagnant connections to legacy VLANs and layer 1 physical connections.

- **Logical Routing**: NSX provides dynamic routing within logical switches, and also between multiple virtual networks.

- **Logical Firewall**: NSX comes bundled with a kernel enabled distributed firewall to safe guard the virtual network, which helps in securing the network, and also provides features such as performance, activity monitoring, and micro segmentation.

- **Sticky Rules**: Security policies and rules assigned to a virtual machine are sticked to them – even if they are migrated to other hosts. This is often impossible in physical network setups.

- **Logical Load Balancer**: NSX features fully functional load balancers which can be terminated via SSH.

- **Logical VPN**: NSX also virtualizes and implements VPN functionalities in the virtual network. It offers site to site and remote access VPN services.

- **NSX API**: NSX's RESTful API provides integration of NSX into any other cloud management platform besides VMware, including OpenStack. However, it can be used within the VMware architecture as well.

NSX is a feature rich data center solution for network virtualization. It offers great flexibility and a bundle of services, which improve the overall performance of the network and the whole data center as well. Its primary use is in automating a data center by increasing the speed of network provisioning process, and by offering simple solution for additional virtual or physical hardware installation. It also helps to streamline modifying or creating DMZs in a network. In other words, if you plan to optimize security and micro-segmentation, NSX can be interesting.

NSX is a great tool when deploying of application is required with the aid of automated networks, and to isolate the testing environments from production environments, which is very complex process otherwise.

NSX components

To understand NSX better, we will break into its subcomponents and understand each one of the components that together make NSX. Following image shows the NXS components:

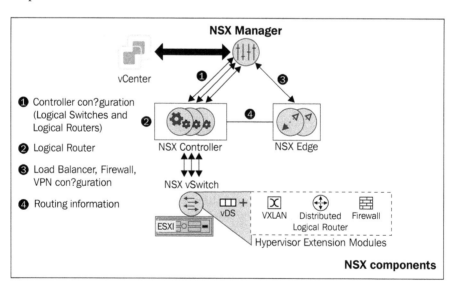

NSX components

Major components of NSX are as follows:

- **NSX manager**: NSX manager is a virtual appliance and can be installed on any ESXi host in the virtual environment managed by vCenter Server. NSX manager is the centralized management console for NSX and gives a unified collated description of the whole network. Note that NSX is no replacement for standard or distributed virtual switches, it is more of a capability extension for them. NSX makes use of **Virtual Extensible LAN (VXLAN)** to span layer 2 segments inside tunnels between ESXi hosts, without using multiple stretched VLANs.

- **NSX vSwitch**: As the name suggests, this is the virtual switch component of NSX and it bridges the gap between the virtual servers and the actual physical network hardware, allowing communication to take place smoothly.

- **NSX Controller**: NSX controller is the central control plane for the network topologies in the data center. Major part of NSX controller's tasks involves controlling NSX virtual switches and keeping a database of information pertaining to all virtual machines, hosts, logical switches, and VXLANs.

- **NSX Edge Gateway**: NSX Edge Gateway is responsible for bringing security and gateway services to the NSX tool, which helps to control and isolate the network from outside network. It is sort of creating a private restricted network. NSX Edge can be used as a distributed/logical router or as a services gateway. When installed as a logical router, it allows NSX to have east-west distributed routing capabilities. In case NSX edge is being used as a services gateway, it is used to connect isolated networks to uplink networks by giving them common gateway services such as DHCP, NAT, VPN, and so on. Also, hosts not integrated in the virtual infrastructure can use NSX services by using the NSX Edge Gateway as their gateway.

- **NSX Distributed Firewall**: NSX comes bundled with a kernel embedded firewall, which enables NSX to have more control over network performance and traffic flow. Security policies can be created for this firewall using vCenter Server for data centers, clusters, hosts, and so on. This firewall is very efficient as it adjusts its own resource utilization and capacity depending on the hosts it needs to monitor. It also adjusts the sizing whenever a new host is added or an existing host is turned off on purpose.

Deploying NSX Manager

NSX Manager centrally manages NSX, and is installed and run as a virtual appliance on an ESXi host. NSX Manager should not be installed on any of the clusters it is being used to manage. Instead, a dedicated cluster for management should be commissioned separately.

One NSX Manager is used to manage only one single vCenter Server setup. Both the Linux appliance and the Windows variant are supported along with the NSX Manager. The NSX manager is responsible for controlling and managing the whole virtual network and therefore it is crucially important to prevent any unplanned outages on the host it is installed on. High Availability and DRS are highly recommended to avoid any failures, and to amplify the resilience of the management appliance. All planned maintenance operations need to be performed only after migrating the host to some other functional host via vMotion.

Steps for installing NSX Manager

NSX Manager is installed as an OVF template. Following steps need to be taken to install/deploy NSX manager in a VMware environment:

1. In the vCenter Server, select **Cluster** and under the **Actions** menu, select **Deploy OVF template**.
2. In the dialog box, browse and select **OVF template** for NSX Manager.
3. Review details and accept the EULA.
4. Select the name and folder of the applicable cluster.
5. Choose the desired storage cluster where the manager needs to be installed.
6. Choose the VM network which will be used to manage the NSX Manager.
7. Finish the setup to complete the installation.

Data center access layer deployment

Deployment of a virtual network in a scalable network structure involves a lot of planning and strategizing, in order to cause zero or minimal impact on any current services. Any virtualization of network involves the following three main practices:

- Uncoupling
- Reproducing
- Automating

If all these three points are kept in consideration, the resulting network should be efficient as desired.

Logical routing

NSX platform supports two modes of routing. In this section, we will learn about the two supported routing modes in NSX and how they can be used in some common routing topologies.

Distributed routing

Distributed routing in the NSX platform offers optimized and scalable way of handling all communications between virtual machines and all resources with the same data center. This communication flow is also known as East – West traffic within a data center. Usually, the amount of east west traffic in any data center is huge and is expected to grow with time.

Centralized routing

Centralized routing can also be used under the NSX platform with the aid of the NSX Edge services router, which provides traditional centralized routing support. Apart from centralized routing service, NSX edge services router also provides a bundle of services like NAT, DHCP, load balancing, and north-south traffic.

Logical routing makes use of various components on the NSX platform. As a whole, all the components under NSX have a role to play, but the major components responsible for implementing logical routing successfully are:

- NSX Manager
- Logical router control virtual machine
- Logical router kernel module
- Controller cluster
- NSX edge services router

Logical switching

NSX offers the administrators the ability to spin up logical isolated Layer 2 networks with the same flexibility and functionalities as a virtual machine. Logical switching makes use of three components of NSX while switching and communicating. These three components are:

- **NSX Manager**: As discussed earlier in this chapter, NSX manager is the management plane that is used to configure local switches, and connect multiple virtual machines to the local switches configured with NSX. NSX manager also offers an API interface, which eases out the administrator's task of automating deployment and managing these switches.

- **Controller cluster**: The Controller cluster in NSX is the control plane and its primary role is to manage the switching and routing modules in hypervisors. The controller cluster is also used to manage few logical switches with the use of its controller nodes, which are present by default. With the use of controller cluster to manage VXLAN based logical switches, the need of multicast support over physical hardware is eliminated, and the administrator can reap the benefits of NSX without any hassles from the physical network infrastructure.

- **UWA and VTEP**: **User World Agent** (**UWA**) and **VXLAN Tunnel Endpoint** (**VTEP**) are the two types of data place components on a hypervisor, which allow communication between the controller cluster, other hypervisors, and physical hardware, by providing the path and means of communication. UWA is primarily responsible for establishing and maintaining a connection with the controller cluster, while VTEP creates tunnels among hypervisors for efficient communication and data transfers.

While preparing the NSX platform for logical switching, the controller cluster and hypervisors need to be deployed and configured using NSX Manager component. Post this, logical switching components need to be configured, and then the span of logical switches needs to be defined, which is done by creating a transport zone. Administrators can add clusters or sets of clusters in this transport zone. A logical switch can then span the data of these clusters which are listed in the transport zone. Installing an Edge services router in the infrastructure will bring features to amplify the network's agility. It is majorly responsible for providing the logical switches access to WAN, logical IP addressing, switch addressing with or without NAT services, and so on.

Logical firewalls

VMware NSX comes with a prepackaged, inbuilt, distributed, kernel-based firewalling. It brings a lot of features to the NSX platform, such as activity monitoring, line rate performance, and many more. These features are in addition to all the basic features a firewall has to offer. We will cover few key benefits or key features logical firewall in NSX has to offer.

Network isolation

Network isolation is one of the key steps in moving towards a secure network. It is the first move in implementing network security and can be used in multiple scenarios, such as separating production network from test or developer network, or meeting the compliance standards. In traditional infrastructures, access control lists along with firewall rules and policies on the hardware devices were used to enable isolation in a network. Virtual networks are however easy to configure for isolation as they are isolated because of their separation from the physical network. Every virtual network when created is isolated, and it remains isolated unless it is configured or a connection is established with external network or peers.

Network segmentation

Network virtualization makes network segmentation comparatively easy. Network segmentation is based and carried out on the same concept as network isolation, but it is applied inside a multitier network. In general terms, segmentation is the process of allowing or denying traffic between network segments with the use of a physical router or a Firewall configured to do exactly that. VMware NSX offers network segmentation to empower the virtual network infrastructure in any virtual environment.

Every virtual network supports multi-tier network environment, and can have multiple layer 2 network segments with layer 3 network segmentation or other combinations. For example, a web portal based network may have an application segment, a web segment, and a database segment which can be configured and controlled by NSX. ACLs and firewalls provide segmentation features which are widely in use across the global networks, and are also compliant to the security norms laid as per industry standards. NSX pursues the same compliance and policies, and provides the same output as any physical network based segmentation.

Logical load balancing

Load balancing is one of the most important services in any network architecture. VMware NSX provides seamless and agile load balancing. Load balancing distributes workload across different servers and resources in order to not burden a single one; this also helps in ensuring the high availability of applications.

NSX load balancing service is flexible and is specifically designed with cloud applications in focus. It can be customized as per different environmental requirements and is fully programmable with the help of its API. NSX load balancing offers the following two modes of support while interacting with the applications hosted on the NSX managed virtual infrastructure:

- Arms mode
- Transparent mode

Summary

In this chapter, we discussed the NSX product family and its benefits when used along with vSphere. NSX is a new and incredibly powerful tool for creating and managing virtual networks. Especially in combination with vSphere, NSX-v offers the most advanced features, including dynamic routing, load balancing, and VPN gateways for flexible and scalable virtual infrastructure setups. On the other hand, NSX-MH offers great integration possibilities for customers interested in cloud setups with open-source tools like OpenStack or CloudStack, and alternative hypervisors such as KVM and XEN. Network virtualization makes heavy use of VXLAN technology which encapsulates tunneled virtual machine traffic between hypervisors and integrated networking components. To implement a secure infrastructure we're able to use distributed virtual firewalls and apply security policies on particular virtual machines. The core component of NSX is an appliance that can be easily deployed using vCenter Server.

Anyway, network virtualization is a very complex topic that needs to be planned and designed carefully to ensure implementing an efficient way to improve workload management.

In the next chapter, we will have a deeper look at virtual storage. We will learn how to configure, maintain, and use storage along with vSphere. Especially, we will have a deeper look at data stores, and how they can be used and maintained.

6
Managing Virtual Storage

In the previous chapter, we discussed network virtualization with VMware NSX. We covered and understood how the product variants NSX-v and NSX-MH can help us to provide a dynamic and scalable infrastructure setup to match our business' requirements. Distributed virtual firewalls and sticky security rules can be used to harden the virtual infrastructure.

This chapter covers basics of virtual storage and discusses two of the major file systems used in the VMware environment. We will also learn how to configure storage and to manage datastores in the most efficient way, for optimizing storage performance in a virtual environment. Data handling is one of the crucial aspects of storage; hence by the end of this module you will be able to know how to manage data, how to backup data, and about data deduplication and recovery. You will be able to understand and work with virtual storage in a VMware vSphere environment. In this chapter, we'll be covering the following topics:

- Understanding virtual storage, datastores, and file systems
- Managing and configuring datastores
- vSphere Storage API for Data Protection
- vSphere Data Protection Appliances – managing data backup and recovery

Understanding virtual storage, datastores, and file systems

In any data center, physical or virtual, storage is considered to be the most critical and crucial aspect, because the main purpose of any server or information system is to manage and effectively store data for future retrieval. VMware vSphere offers flexible storage systems to fit in requirements for almost every kind of virtual infrastructure setup.

Having multiple options to choose from gives the storage administrator freedom to setup storage systems as per their personalized needs based on costs, performance, and requirements. Shared storage for multiple reasons is considered to be better than traditional storage solutions as it is enabled using advanced features, such as disaster recovery, high availability, virtual machine migration, and so on.

Ideally, VMware ESXi hosts are configured in such a manner that they all have access to datastores. A datastore is a logical storage container that conceals the individual specifications of storage devices and provides a collaborative single module for storing virtual machine files. The file system to be used on a datastore usually depends on the type of storage. For local discs or SAN arrays you might choose VMFS, for NAS systems and network shares NFS is a possible solution.

VMware vSphere offers flexible choices for storage solutions. A few of the most commonly used and best storage options most data centers choose are:

- **Direct Attached Storage**: As the name suggests, it refers to the storage devices directly connected to the ESXi server instead of a network connection. These storage devices use a physical connection to transmit data to and from hosts.

- **Fibre Channel**: Fiber channel is a high-speed data transfer link established between the ESXi hosts and the storage system. It transmits SCSI commands from one fiber channel node to another. Multiple nodes or storage systems are connected using a fiber channel switch.

- **FCoE**: Fiber channel over Ethernet (FCoE) encapsulates the traffic over a fiber channel into frames, which are then merged into network traffic. By merging the network traffic and FCoE frame data, it increases the utilization of physical infrastructure.

- **iSCSI**: iSCSI consists of a iSCSI storage system on which one or more LUNs are created and are accessed over the normal Ethernet network. It works in a similar way as fiber channel, except that in fiber channel it has fiber channel switches while in iSCSI, normal ethernet switches are used instead. This makes iSCSI a very cost-effective alternative to expensive fiber-channel storage systems.

- **NAS**: **Network Attached Storage** (**NAS**) is a file level data storage, which is used to provide data access to its clients. ESXi supports the NFS file system; the NFS server contains directories which can be mounted on ESXi hosts to be used as shared storage.

Datastores

Datastores are logical storage units formed by either; one storage server, or spanning across multiple storage servers or devices. Datastores are used to store virtual machine files, ISO images, virtual machine templates, and floppy images.

Datastores are analogous to file systems and hide specifics of each storage device. They also provide a collaborative platform for storage. Depending on the type of storage you use, datastores can be backed by the following file system formats:

- **Virtual Machine File System (VMFS)**
- **Network File System (NFS)**

Both these file systems support access to multiple ESXi hosts simultaneously, which we will see in the following sections. On the other hand, it is also possible to pass particular LUNs directly into virtual machines. In this case, ESXi just passes the LUN, and no dedicated file system is used in between. Some special applications such as **Microsoft Cluster Services** (**MSCS**) or SAN management applications require low-level access to storage. This mechanism called **Raw Device Mapping** (**RDM**) offers two modes:

- **Pass-through mode**: ESXi passes all SCSI commands to the storage; no virtual disk features are available. This mode is also called physical compatibility as mapped LUNs act like they do on physical servers.
- **Non-pass-through mode**: This mode is also called virtual compatibility and offers the ability of using the LUN like a virtual disk. This also enables the usage of snapshots.

If a particular LUN is mapped to a virtual machine, a mapping file is created on the VMFS datastore it resides in. Physical compatibility mappings will create a `name-rdmp.vmdk` file, while `name-rdm.vmdk` files can identify virtual compatibility mappings. A mapping file acts like a proxy to the physical LUN, so in the virtual machine's configuration, no SCSI path but the mapping file is referenced. This enables the hypervisor to react on path changes, for example, link failures in a Fibre-channel based setup. It does that without harming the virtual machine.

Datastores can be added to a datastore cluster. A datastore cluster is a collection of multiple datastores with a common shared management interface and resources. With the use of datastore clusters, the administrator can also use Storage DRS for managing storage resources more effectively and efficiently.

VMFS datastores

VMFS is VMware's proprietary file system and is a special high performance file system which is optimized for storing virtual machines and their files. It also offers additional features for cluster setups such as file locking.

To set up a VMFS based datastore, the vSphere Web Client is used for all storage blocks discovered by an ESXi host. VMFS datastores can be extended by spanning multiple physical storage units, including SAN storage and local storage. Spanning storage across multiple devices offers the administrator the flexibility to create datastores for virtual machines as per requirements. VMFS datastore's storage capacity can be increased or decreased even while the virtual machines are running, which helps in no downtime during the process.

Several versions of VMFS file systems are available on the market. Currently the version in use is VMFS-5. vSphere 5.x or 6.0 supports VMFS version 3 and 5. ESXi can format any SCSI based storage system as a VMFS file system. The primary role of a VMFS file system is to store virtual machine files. A single ESXi host can have up to 256 VMFS datastores with a maximum size of 64TB per volume. The minimum size of a VMFS datastore is 1.3GB but the recommended size from VMware is 2GB. Multiple virtual machines can be stored at the same VMFS datastore, and multiple virtual machines can access the same VMFS datastore at the same time without any issues. A single VMFS volume can be shared across multiple ESXi hosts and a single VMFS datastore can be connected to up to 64 ESXi hosts.

The following table shows major differences between the three VMFS versions:

	VMFS-2	**VMFS-3**	**VMFS-5**
Supported by	ESX 2.x, ESXi 3.x/4.x (read-only)	ESX(i) 3.x and higher	ESX(i) 5.x and higher
Block size(s)	1, 8, 64 or 256 MB	1, 2, 4 or 8 MB	1 MB (fixed)
Maximum file size	1 MB block size: 456 MB 8 MB: 2.5 TB 64 MB: 28.5 TB 256 MB: 64 TB	1 MB block size: 256 GB 2 MB: 512 GB 4 MB: 1 TB 8 MB: 2 TB	62 TB
Files per volume	Ca. 256 (no directories supported)	Ca. 30,720	Ca. 130,690

Using a shared storage system has the following advantages:

- **High Availability (HA)**: VMware HA increases availability for applications running in virtual machines by reacting on ESXi host failures. VMware HA eliminates the use of any dedicated standby hardware or any additional software. If a virtual machine protected by HA crashes, it is restarted as fast as possible on an alternative node.

- **DRS / storage DRS**: VMware distributed resource scheduler is used for dynamically balancing the computing load across the hosts in the cluster. DRS constantly monitors the load of all the hosts in the cluster. VMware DRS can automatically allocate additional resources by distributing the virtual machines across the hosts in the cluster. Storage DRS is used for balancing storage loads and usage, which can reduce IO peaks that slow the workloads.

- **vMotion / Storage vMotion**: vMotion is the process of migrating a virtual machine from one ESXi host to another while the virtual machine is powered on. DRS uses vMotion to balance load throughout the host in the virtual machine. Storage vMotion enables virtual machines to be migrated between datastores without shutting down the particular workload.

- **Storage I/O Control (SIOC)**: First introduced with ESXi 4.1, this technology ensures that virtual machines on multiple ESXi hosts and sharing storage will consume the same fair amount of resources. This prevents particular VMs consuming more resources, forcing other workloads to have poor I/O performances (noisy neighbor scenario). Storage I/O control is enabled per datastore. It monitors the average latency and adjusts the particular virtual machine's virtual disk device queues to ensure fair I/O resource consumption. By default, the threshold is set to 30ms. As these settings are applied at datastore level, online migrations are also unable to harm fair resource consumption. In combination with I/O operations per second (IOPS) limitations per virtual machine level, this technology can ensure that prioritized workloads always get the resources they need.

- **Datastore Heartbeating**: To make vSphere clusters even more resilient, datastores can be used in addition to network connections for heartbeat communication. By default, particular ESXi hosts communicate with each other to ensure that all nodes are up and running, using network sockets. If one of the nodes crashes, the other nodes will recognize this and restart the affected virtual machines if they were protected by HA. Datastore Heartbeating enables ESXi cluster communication using shared storage to avoid a cluster split in case of a complete network failure. If this issue arises, the ESXi hosts communicate using files on datastores. It is recommended to enable this feature. The default is to use between 2 and 5 datastores for cluster communication. If enabled, a directory **.vSphere-HA** is created on every datastore; for every cluster a subfolder is created. These directories should not be deleted manually. The datastore usage for this feature is between 3 MB to 2 GB.

NFS datastores

ESXi can access a particular NFS volume located on a NAS server. The administrator can mount the NFS volume on to the ESXi host. NFS datastores can be used to keep virtual machine, template files, and ISO images. It is often used as a cost-effective alternative to SCSI based shared storage. It is often used along with NAS systems.

ESXi supports the following storage capabilities on NFS volumes:

- As discussed in the previous section, vMotion is the process of migrating a virtual machine from one ESXi host to another while the virtual machine is powered on
- VMware DRS and HA
- ISO images which are present as optical media to virtual machines
- Virtual machine snapshots

The NFS storage keeps in consideration that the maximum size of a datastore is the maximum size supported by the NFS server; ESXi doesn't impose any size limitations. While vSphere 5.5 supports NFS version 3, the most recent version 6.0 also supports NFS 4.1. NFS 4.1 provides better locking mechanisms, along with performance and security features. In addition to storing virtual machines on NFS datastores, you can also use NFS as a central repository for your ISO images, virtual machine files, templates, and so on.

To use NFS, the administrator needs to create a directory on the NFS server and then mount it as a datastore on all the ESXi hosts. If you wish to use the NFS datastore as an ISO repository, the administrator can connect the virtual machine CD ROM device to an ISO file on the NFS datastore and can install the guest operating system from the ISO.

Managing and configuring datastores

In this section of the chapter, we will look at how to create, upgrade, increase, and mount VMFS datastores.

Creating a VMFS datastore using vSphere Web Client

VMFS datastores are used to store virtual machine files, as discussed previously. VMFS datastores can be setup on any SCSI based storage technology like fiber-channel, iSCSI, or local storage. VMFS datastores can be created from the vSphere Web Client by performing the following steps:

1. Click **Create New Datastore** icon and type the datastore name.

2. Select VMFS location and choose VMFS as the datastore type.

3. Select **LUN** to be used as the datastore. It might be necessary to scan the ESXi for new LUNs first; this can be done under the **Configure** and **Storage adapters** pane by clicking **Rescan**.

4. Specify the partitioning information.

5. In case of VMFS3 version, select the maximum file size and click **Finish** to complete the creation of VMFS datastore.

Creating an NFS datastore in vSphere Web Client

1. Create the **New Datastore** icon.

2. Type the name of the datastore.

3. Select the datastore type (Network File System).

4. Type the server name and mount point folder name. Instead of server name, we can also use the IP address and name of the NAS server.

5. Select NFS mount point.

6. If you are creating a datastore in the data center or at the cluster level, select the host that requires access to that datastore.

Upgrading a VMFS datastore

If the current version of VMFS datastores used is either version 2 or 3, then they can be upgraded to VMFS version 5. Upgrading VMFS 2 datastores to VMFS 5 is a two step process; firstly involving, upgrading from VMFS 2 to VMFS 3, and then upgrading to VMFS 5 from VMFS 3.

To upgrade from VMFS 2 to VMFS 3, you will need a legacy host running ESX version 2.x. Execute the following steps:

1. Shutdown all virtual machines residing on the affected storage.
2. Create a full backup of the datastore.
3. Ensure that no other ESX host accesses the datastore.
4. Ensure that the block size does not exceed 8 MB as VMFS-3 only supports block sizes up to 8 MB.
5. Connect to the ESX host using the vSphere legacy client as vCenter Server does not support ESX 2.x hosts.
6. Click **Configuration** and **Storage** and select the affected datastore.
7. Click on **Upgrade to VMFS3**.
8. Check for new VMFS volumes on all other nodes that also have access to the upgraded VMFS volume.

The VMFS 3 to VMFS 5 upgrade can be performed even while the virtual machines are running on the datastore. While upgrading from VMFS 3 to 5, the ESXi host preserves all the files on the datastore. The upgrade is a one-way process and cannot be restored back to its previous version. Please keep in mind that upgrading VMFS from 3 to 5 does not change the block size; as a result, you will not be able to create files such as virtual disks bigger than 2 TB. It is highly recommended that you reformat VMFS volumes instead of upgrading them. A VMFS datastore can be upgraded to VMFS 5 using the vSphere Web Client by following these steps:

1. Click on the datastore to upgrade and go to **Settings** under the **Manage** tab.
2. Click **Upgrade to VMFS5**.
3. Verify the host accessing the datastore, supports VMFS5.
4. Click **OK** to start the upgrade.

Increasing the VMFS datastore's capacity

An administrator can dynamically increase the size of a VMFS datastore by increasing the size or by adding a new extent. You can use one of the following methods for increasing the size of a datastore.

- **Dynamically growing a datastore**: If there is some free size available on the LUN.
- **Dynamically adding a new extent**: A particular datastore can have 32 extents. The spanned VMFS datastore can use one or all of its extents at one time.

Increasing the VMFS datastore's size using vSphere Web Client

When you need to add virtual machines to a datastore, or when virtual machines already running on the datastore require more space, the administrator can dynamically add/increase the size of the VMFS datastore using the following steps:

1. Select the datastore to grow and select the **Increase datastore capacity** icon.
2. Select the device from the list of storage devices.
   - Your selection would depend on whether we are expanding an existing extent or are we adding a new extent.
3. Renew the current disk layout to see available configurations and select **Next**.
4. Select the configuration option on the basis of the following options:
   - Use free space to add new extent
   - Use free space to expand existing extent
   - Use free space
   - Use all available partitions
5. Set the capacity of the extent and finish.

Unmounting and mounting a VMFS datastore

When the administrator unmounts the datastore, it remains intact, but can no longer be seen from the host that you specify. To avoid data loss, this is necessary before maintenance tasks on the storage system can be executed. The datastore is still available and accessible to other ESXi hosts where it remains mounted. A datastore can be mounted to, or unmounted from, different hosts in order to provide or revoke access to the storage. The datastore remains intact and accessible to other hosts.

Before unmounting the datastore, make sure that the following prerequisites are met:

- No virtual machine resides on the datastore
- The datastore is not a part of any datastore cluster
- The datastore is not managed by Storage DRS
- Storage I/O control is disabled on the datastore
- Datastore is not used by HA Heartbeat

To unmount the datastore, please follow these steps:

1. Right-click the datastore and select **Unmount datastore**.
2. If the datastore is shared, specify which host should no longer access the datastore and provide confirmation.

An unmounted datastore can be mounted by following these steps:

1. Right-click the datastore to mount and select the **Mount datastore** option.
2. Select the hosts that should access the datastore.

Removing a VMFS datastore

An administrator can remove any kind of datastore. When the administrator deletes a datastore, it destroys and disappears from all ESXi hosts. The following prerequisites need to be considered before removing a VMFS datastore:

- Remove or migrate all virtual machines from the datastore
- Make sure that no other host is accessing this particular datastore
- Disable Storage DRS and Storage I/O Control
- Make sure that the datastore is not used by HA Heartbeat

The following steps need to be taken while removing the VMFS Datastore:

1. Right-click on the datastore and select **All vCenter actions**.

2. Select **Delete Datastore** and confirm the deletion.

vSphere Storage APIs for Data Protection (VADP)

After a period of time, the VMware vSphere environment might undergo some changes; hence it is advisable to back up the vSphere environment. It is recommended not to use traditional backup methods in a virtualized environment to take backups of your virtual machines. The disadvantages of using traditional backup methods in a virtualized environment include:

- License costs for the used backup solution

- High ESXi host resource utilization

- Longer duration for the backup process

- Slower recovery process

- Increase in storage capacity requirement

- Need to install a backup agent onto the virtual machines

Backing up virtual machines requires backup solutions that can leverage virtualization architecture. In this section, we will learn about what feature VMware provides when taking backup of your virtual machines or while managing data in an efficient way.

vSphere Storage APIs for Data Protection (VADP) is a framework that enables you to implement agent-free backups of virtual machines in an efficient and centralized way. Products using this API are able to use proven virtual machine snapshot mechanisms to create backups and transfer data to backup servers. As a result, backup products are able to perform nondisruptive backup processes without stopping particular workloads. As most products using VADP are also integrated into vCenter Server, backup and restore is an easy task that administrators can control from their everyday administration tool. Restoring jobs can use virtual machine operations such as creating and cloning to provide fast restores. VADP is fully integrated into the vSphere framework and therefore needs no additionally installed software components. It is also enabled on all licensed vSphere editions such as Standard, Enterprise, and Enterprise Plus – the free version of ESXi is not eligible to use the API.

Data deduplication

Data deduplication reduces the amount of storage capacity required for backups and reduces the total cost of ownership for data protection. Data deduplication means that the backup operation:

- Evaluates the blocks that will be saved

- Compares them to blocks that have been saved

- Identifies the blocks containing identical data

- Stores only the changed blocks; this feature is also called **Changed Block Tracking (CBT)**

The storage blocks with the same information as the previous backup will not be stored twice. VDP uses a deduplicated storage in the backend. Data deduplication is used by a lot of companies providing backup solutions, for example EMC Avamar. VDP is also based on the patented EMC Avamar technology. In this chapter, we will be focusing on VMware backup solution.

Data deduplication, in general, can be performed at both hardware and software level, and a combined approach provides an optimal fine result. Data deduplication can be done using the following two techniques:

- **Post-process deduplication**: The deduplication process occurs after the data is written on the storage device.

- **In-line deduplication**: Data deduplication is done when the data enters the storage device in real time. This is more efficient than post-process deduplication as data isn't stored and deduplicated afterwards.

vSphere Data Protection Appliance

Backup is the process of copying and archiving the data so that it can be used to restore the original data if the data is lost. In vSphere environments, the vSphere Data Protection (VDP) appliance is an efficient and feature-rich tool for backup and restore. In this section, we will have a deeper look at managing backup and restore scenarios with VDP.

VDP is fully integrated with vCenter Server and provides agentless, disc-based backups of virtual machines.

It requires no additional software installation because it uses the vSphere Storage API for Data Protection API built inside the ESXi framework. It provides plenty of features, including:

- Backing up the virtual machine guest operating system without creating temporary files in the virtual machine
- Restoring individual files and also application data such as Exchange mailboxes or Microsoft SQL Server databases
- Doing incremental backups

VDP ensures fast and efficient backups of virtual machines even if the virtual machines are powered off. It uses patented technologies such as VADP and CBT to reduce the backup data consumption. It can perform a full virtual machine and file level restore without the need for an agent.

Before deploying VDP, the following requirements need to be met:

- VMware vCenter Server version 5.1 or above
- vSphere Web Client

VDP is deployed as a preconfigured appliance; each appliance supports as many as 100 virtual machines. As many as 10 VDP appliances can be deployed per vCenter Server and one VDP appliance can be used per ESXi host. The VDP 5.x appliance is available in 3 backup storage size configurations: 0.5 TB, 1 TB, and 2 TB. The minimum processor and memory required by a VDP appliance is 4 vCPUs and 4 GB of memory.

Available editions

Prior to vSphere 6.0, VDP was available in two editions: VDP and VDP Advanced (VDPA). The following table lists the differences between VDP and VDP Advanced in vSphere 5.x:

Feature/Edition	VDP	VDP Advanced (VDPA)
Licensing	Part of vSphere Essentials Plus and above	Licensed per CPU or part of vSphere with Operations Management Enterprise and above
Maximum supported VMs per appliance	100	400
Maximum appliances per vCenter	10	

Feature/Edition	VDP	VDP Advanced (VDPA)
Maximum deduplicated storage	0.5 TB, 1 TB or 2 TB	Dynamic, up to 8 TB
File system level backup and restore	Yes	
Support for Microsoft SQL Server and Exchange	No	Yes

Beginning with vSphere 6.0, VMware simplified VDP by merging the advanced features with the formerly conventional backup appliance. Beyond that, VDP now also offers better support for EMC Data Domain storage systems.

Deploying and configuring VDP

As VDP is provided as an appliance, we only need to download and deploy an OVA file to install it. Follow the steps listed next to deploy VDP:

1. Login using vSphere Web Client.
2. Select an ESXi host from the inventory and click **Deploy OVF Template** in the **Actions** menu.
3. Select the downloaded OVA file and proceed to the next step.
4. Review the OVA details and accept the license agreement.
5. Enter a VM name and select a cluster or ESXi host.
6. Select a datastore and the provisioning type.
7. Define a network to use and enter networking information such as IP address, netmask, DNS servers, and default gateway.
8. Review the configuration details and start deployment.

After deploying VDP, the virtual machine is turned on and configured using a web browser, once the system has booted. In case the appliance's network configuration is invalid and needs to be altered, perform the following steps:

1. Access the appliance console.
2. Select the menu item **Configure Network**.
3. Follow the instructions on the screen to reset the network configuration.
4. Reboot the virtual machine.

The following screenshot demonstrates the appliance's console after boot:

```
**************************************************************************
Welcome to the vSphere Data Protection 6.0 appliance. Version: 6.0.0.190

Quickstart Guide: (How to get VDP running quickly)

  1 - Open a browser to:  https://10.4.14.8:8543/vdp-configure
  2 - Review the Network Settings
  3 - Enter the Time Zone
  4 - Enter the VDP credentials
  5 - Enter the vCenter Registration information
  6 - Click Test Connection
  7 - Click Finish

**************************************************************************

 *Login                               Use Arrow Keys to navigate
  Configure Network                   and <ENTER> to select your choice.
  Set Timezone (Current:PDT)
```

To configure VDP, open a web browser and enter `https://<VDP IP or FQDN>:8543/vdp-configure`.

The default password for root is `changeme`. A wizard will be started, guiding you through the initial configuration of VDP. You need to enter the following information:

- **Network settings** – Such as IP address, netmask, hostname, domain, and so on.
- **Time zone** – Example, Europe/Berlin.
- **Password** – New password for the root user; it must fulfill various password complexity rules.
- **vCenter login credentials** – The account information is used for linking the appliance against vCenter Server. It is advisable to create a dedicated service user for VDP on SSO or the authorization directory.
- **VDP license** – If using VDP 5.x, the administrator can choose between the variant included in vSphere or enter a VDP Advanced license key.
- **Storage** – A new backup storage is created in this step. This storage can be up to 8 TB depending on the VDP edition (prior to VDP 6.x). It is also possible to attach a previously created VDP storage – example, during migrations.

- **Device Allocation** – A storage provisioning type such as Thick or Thin Provisioning is chosen.
- **CPU and Memory** – It is possible to alter the appliance's CPU and memory configuration to fulfill the infrastructure's requirements; bigger environments might need more resources.

After completing the wizard, the appliance is rebooted. You will notice a new icon vSphere Data Protection in vSphere Web Client. As VDP does not support the vSphere legacy client, you will need to use Web Client for using VDP functions. After accessing the appliance's URL the administrator is lead into an administration cockpit, that can be used for controlling the particular appliance's core services. It is also possible to execute an upgrade of the appliance software.

By clicking the **vSphere Data Protection** icon inside vSphere Web Client, a pane including several management tasks is opened. After connecting to your VDP appliance, you're able to:

- Create and modify backup jobs
- Backup and restore particular virtual machines
- Validate integrity of backups
- Monitor storage capacity and last backups of all protected virtual machines
- Configure advanced functions, such as email reporting

Data backup

Creating backup jobs control the backing up virtual machines. To create a backup job, perform the following steps:

1. Switch to the Backup pane in vSphere Web Client after connecting to your VDP appliance.
2. Click **New**.
3. Select all virtual machines that should be protected.
4. Choose a time schedule such as **Daily** or **Weekly performed every <day>**.
5. Configure a retention policy. This policy defines how long backups are retained; after this time frame is exceeded, the backups are deleted.
6. Enter a name for the backup job.
7. Review the configuration and acknowledge creation.

Backup jobs are executed automatically, based on their time frame configuration (example, at night). It is also possible to start backup jobs manually. As VDP offers backup job monitoring, it is easy to recognize failed backups and restart them.

Data recovery

The restore of an entire virtual machine can be performed using VMware vSphere Web Client. The administrator can look at the list of backed up virtual machines and select any of the particular restore points. Backing up the virtual machines in the conventional way, using third-party backup agents, is also possible but not very comfortable and efficient.

Whenever a restore is initiated, VDP is able to find out which blocks have been modified since the chosen restore point, using VADP technology, and recovers only those blocks. This reduces the amount of data transfer in a vSphere environment and time taken for data recovery, decreases.

Using VDP, the administrator can restore specific files and folders in the virtual machine. A file level restore is performed using the vSphere Data Protection restore client. This process enables the end user to perform a restore without the help of any administrator. The end user can select a restore point, browse through the file system, and restore the specific files.

To restore a virtual machine, perform the following steps:

1. Switch to the **Restore** pane in vSphere Web Client after connecting to your VDP appliance.
2. Select the virtual machine you want to restore.
3. Select a backup point.
4. Click **Restore** to open a wizard.
5. If required, choose a dedicated datastore and virtual machine name for the restored virtual machine. It is also possible to overwrite the current virtual machine by checking **Restore to Original Location**.
6. Review your choices.

Afterwards, the virtual machine is restored.

Summary

In this chapter, we have covered the basics of virtual storage in a vSphere environment and become aware of the two major file systems being used in the VMware environment. We know that VMFS is VMware's proprietary cluster-aware file system for SCSI-based storage. Along with NAS systems or file servers, we can also use NFS shares to store virtual machines and other files, such as ISO files and templates.

Now that we are well versed with the data handling techniques in a virtual environment, we know how to manage backing up and restoring data, and use **Changed Block Tracking** (**CBT**) to use storage more efficiently. For backing up virtual machines, we can use **vSphere Data Protection** (**VDP**), which is available with no additional cost in all commercial vSphere editions, or other third-party products using the vSphere Storage API for Data Protection (VADP). Using this appliance, we can easily create and restore backups using vSphere Web Client.

In the next chapter, we will be learning about a new product called vSAN for effectively providing high-performance shared storage. vSAN has been introduced as a part of vSphere for the first time in vSphere 5.5 and offers more flexibility and options to manage storage.

7

Working with VSAN

In previous chapter, we discussed basics of virtual storage in a vSphere environment and discussed two of the major file systems used in the VMware environment. We learnt how to configure storage and to manage datastores in the most efficient way, for optimizing storage performance in a virtual environment. In the end, we learnt process of data management, data backup, data deduplication, and recovery.

Now, in this chapter, we will cover the implementation and configuration of **Virtual SAN (VSAN)** with vSphere. VSAN has been introduced with vSphere 5.5 for the first time to manage storage in an easier way, while reducing storage costs. We will be covering VSAN, and its implementation and configuration. This chapter also covers how to deploy and change a VM with storage policies and failure resilience with VSAN. Following is the list of topics we will go through in this chapter:

- An overview of Virtual SAN
- Installing and configuring Virtual SAN
- Deploying and changing a virtual machine with storage policies
- Failure resilience with VSAN

An overview of Virtual SAN

With the release of vSphere 5.5, VMware introduced **software-defined data center (SDDC)** capabilities for the first time. One of these new features is called VMware Virtual SAN and it addresses the **software-defined storage (SDS)** philosophy. Virtual SAN is a hybrid storage system that leverages and utilizes locally attached **Solid State Drives (SSDs)** and **Hard Disk Drives (HDDs)**, to provide a high-performance and clustered datastore on which virtual machine files can be stored.

VSAN is fully integrated with vSphere. It is configured as a cluster, so a number of ESXi hosts can be a part of a single VSAN cluster. The ESXi hosts communicate with each other through a dedicated VSAN Network. So, a VMkernel port needs to be created and marked for VSAN. To provide both performant and redundant storage, VSAN makes intense use of SSDs and HDDs attached to ESXi hosts.

VSAN aggregates the locally attached disks on the server into a VSAN cluster, to create a shared storage solution. It is capable of using distributed features, such as **High Availability (HA)**, **Distributed Resource Scheduler (DRS)**, vMotion, and Storage vMotion.

In vSphere 6.0, VSAN was overhauled to enable more cluster nodes and bigger virtual machines. Refer to the following table:

	VSAN 5.5	**VSAN 6**
Hosts in a VSAN cluster	3-32	3-64
Virtual machines per host	100	200
Virtual machines per VSAN cluster	3200	6400
Virtual machine disk size	2032 GB	62 TB
Storage device usage	SSDs as cache, HDDs as datastore	**Hybrid mode**: SSDs as cache, HDDs as datastore **All-Flash mode**: SSDs as cache and datastore

Unlike VSAN 5.5, VSAN 6 also supports setups which only use SSDs, to enable even higher performance for very I/O intensive workloads. In comparison with VSAN 5.5, VSAN 6 All-Flash offers 4.5x more IOPS (90,000 versus. 20,000).

VSAN is often chosen as high-performant and cost-effective alternative to expensive Flash-enabled storage systems. As it is included in VMkernel, it offers less overhead, which results in very good IO performances.

Requirements of VSAN

VSAN offers huge benefits along with immense amount of flexibility and features in the vSphere environment for storage. However, to successfully implement VSAN in a virtual infrastructure, following requirements need to be met:

- **vCenter Server**: VSAN requires vCenter Server 5.5 or higher. It can be managed by both the Windows version of vCenter Server or vCenter Server Appliance. Virtual SAN can only be configured and managed through vSphere Web Client; the vSphere legacy client is not supported.

- **ESXi hosts**: VSAN requires at least 3 or more ESXi hosts to form a vSAN cluster. All the ESXi hosts contribute to the total storage of a VSAN cluster. All ESXi hosts need to have the same version; so for VSAN 6.0, all hosts need to have version 6.0, and if you go for VSAN 5.5, make sure all hosts are running ESXi 5.5.

- **Disk controllers**: Each ESXi host that contributes storage to the Virtual SAN cluster requires a disk controller. This can be a SAS or SATA **host bus adapter (HBA)** or a RAID controller.

- **Hard disk drives**: Each ESXi host should have at least one SAS (Software Attached SCSI), or SATA HDD to participate in a VSAN Cluster. HDDs account for the storage capacity of the VSAN shared storage. Adding more HDDs would increase the overall capacity and improve the virtual machine performance as well. VSAN 6.0 can also be configured in All-Flash mode; as a result only flash resources are used, enabling even better I/O performance.

- **Solid State Drives**: Each ESXi host must have at least one SSD present. Flash based devices provide the read and write cache buffers to the VSAN Cluster. The larger the capacity of the SSDs, the more IO can be cached and greater performance can be achieved. SSDs don't add to the overall capacity of the VSAN datastores; they are only used for caching if VSAN is not configured in All-Flash mode.

- **Network Interface Cards**: Each ESXi host should have at least one 1 GB ethernet or 10 GB ethernet card. We can use multiple NICs for redundancy purpose.

- **Virtual Switch Types**: VSAN is supported on both vNetwork Standard and vNetwork Distributed switches.

- **VMkernel network**: On each ESXi host, a VMkernel port, marked for VSAN traffic, must be created. This new type of VMkernel adapter has been added in vSphere 5.5 and higher.

For the choice of controllers, HDDs, and SSDs, it is important to follow VMware's **Hardware Compatibility List (HCL)** for supported setups. It can be accessed at:

```
http://www.vmware.com/resources/compatibility/search.
php?deviceCategory=vsan.
```

Benefits of using VSAN

VSAN, being the latest in storage virtualization, offers a huge list of benefits to administrators. With the use of VSAN, administrators can create multiple storage profiles for their datacenter/datastores. These storage profiles per datastore allow different virtual machines to run on a different storage.

VSAN can be seamlessly integrated with vCenter Server, which provides more flexibility to the administrators in implementation and configuration of VSAN. VSAN's capabilities are built into vSphere and do not require any appliance, which makes it more efficient. Also, VSAN cluster is quite scalable and an administrator can have up to 32 (VSAN 5.5) or 64 (VSAN 6.0) ESXi hosts in one cluster.

VSAN offers resilience to disk and server failures, and the use of SSD caching on the server improves the overall I/O operations. Running VSAN 6.0 in All-Flash mode offers the maximum of I/O performance possible along with VSAN.

VSAN sizing tool

VMware also offers a free VSAN sizing tool. This tool gives excellent insight to the VSAN architecture. The user needs to provide information about the amount and configuration of virtual machines and ESXi hosts. Once all required information were entered, the utility displays graphic results and reports about possible VSAN configurations. Information listed in the result includes **Disk Space Usage Distribution in GB**, **Virtual SAN Memory Usage**, and so on. This tool helps the administrator to plan the configuration and architecture of the VSAN cluster, and decide on how to configure memory and storage for the cluster. It also helps with calculating infrastructure's costs. The tool is available for free use at `http://virtualsansizing.vmware.com/go/`. Refer to the following screenshot of the webpage:

Installing and configuring VSAN

The process of creating a VSAN cluster is similar to the creation of vSphere HA or DRS clusters. In the previous versions of vSphere, when a cluster object was created in the vCenter inventory, the administrators had the option of vSphere HA or DRS under the **Manage** tab; an option to create a VSAN cluster is located under the same tab.

A VSAN network needs to be added to the host in order to use it. To add a VSAN network, perform the following steps:

1. Select the host and click on the **Add Networking** icon.

2. In the **Add Networking** wizard, select **VMkernel network adapter** and click **Next**.

3. Browse and select the port group. You might create an appropriate port group in advance.

4. Select **Virtual SAN traffic** as the service to be enabled and Click **Next**.

5. Provide the IP information and click **Finish** to add the VSAN network.

The following screenshots demonstrates how to configure a VSAN portgroup using vSphere Web Client:

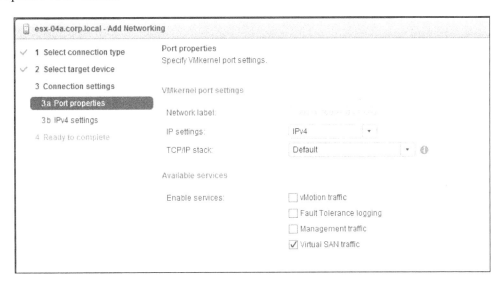

The desired hosts now have the VSAN networking and next, the VSAN cluster needs to be created. To create a VSAN cluster, following steps need to be performed:

1. Select the desired cluster in the vSphere Web Client.

2. Under the **Manage** tab, we have various VSAN options.

3. To enable VSAN cluster, select **General** and click on **Edit**.

4. Select the check box **Turn On Virtual SAN**. The following screenshot shows the VSAN configuration section on a particular cluster in vSphere Web Client:

When VSAN feature is enabled, the administrators can choose whether to add the disks manually or automatically. Refer to the following screenshot:

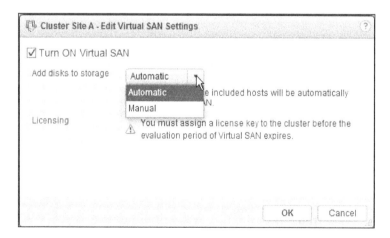

Let's have a deeper look at the two assignment possibilities:

- **Manually adding disks to disk groups**: When the **Manual** option is selected in **Add disk to storage**, the VSAN cluster is created but the size of the storage capacity is zero bytes. The administrator has to manually create disk groups and add at least one magnetic disk and one flash based disk to each disk group. Each disk group can only contain 1 flash based disk and 7 magnetic disks. Every ESXi host in the VSAN cluster can have, at the most, 5 disk groups.

After the disks have been added to disk groups, the size of the VSAN datastore increases according to the capacity of each magnetic disk added to the disk groups.

- **Automatic creation of disk groups**: When the **Automatic** option is selected in **Add disk to storage**, the VSAN system discovers all the local magnetic disks and flash based disks on each ESXi host, and creates a disk group on every ESXi host in the cluster. After the disk groups have been generated, the VSAN shared datastore is created. The size of the shared datastore is equal to the size of all magnetic disks present across all the hosts present in the VSAN cluster.

Virtual SAN datastore properties

The size and capacity of the VSAN shared datastore depends on the capacity and number of magnetic disks per disk group on the ESXi host, and the number of ESXi hosts in the VSAN cluster.

For example, if a VSAN cluster consists of 8 ESXi hosts, each having one disk group of seven magnetic disks of 1 TB in size, the following calculations can be used to figure out the size of the VSAN shared datastore.

Formulas:

```
No. of ESXi hosts * No. of disk groups * No. of HDDs per disk group *
HDD size = Total Raw capacity.

Usable Capacity = Total Raw Capacity - metadata overhead.
```

For metadata overhead, VSAN calculates about 1 GB per disk as a general principle. So, in our example, the total raw capacity would be 56 TB; the usable capacity would be 55.9 TB (56 TB – 56 GB).

After the VSAN shared datastore is created, datastore capabilities based on storage capacity, performance, and availability can be viewed in vCenter Server. These capabilities can be used to create a policy that defines storage requirements of virtual machines. This simplifies the virtual machine provisioning process by giving the power to the administrator to select the correct storage for a particular virtual machine.

The storage is mounted by using **Object Store File System** (**OSFS**). VSAN stores and manages the data in the shared datastores, in form of data containers called as objects. An object is a logical volume that has data and metadata spanned across the cluster.

Virtual machine requirements

When an administrator begins to create and design a virtual machine, the virtual hardware requirement of the particular virtual machine depends on the operating system and the application, which is going to run inside the virtual machine.

The operating system and its applications depend on the virtual CPU, memory, network, and disk allocations. The application might have a set of storage requirements.

The administrator uses a virtual machine storage policy to form a storage capability that will be attached to the virtual machine. Simply, the storage system provides the capabilities and the virtual machine consumes them via requirement placed in the virtual machine policy.

Virtual machine storage policies

Virtual machine storage policies are a set of policies that an administrator can configure on the basis of which applications need to run inside the virtual machine. The storage policies reflect capabilities on the basis of availability, performance, and storage requirement. When a virtual machine is deployed, the administrator can choose the storage policy that meets the creation of the virtual machine's vmdk file.

Virtual machine storage policies were introduced in vSphere 5.0 and were called as vSphere storage profiles. With vSphere storage profiles introduced in 5.0, the capabilities in the policy were used to select the appropriate datastore for the virtual machine. Storage policies introduced with vSphere 5.5 not only select the appropriate datastore for the virtual machines, but also respects preferations regarding performance and availability for a particular virtual machine. This enables administrators to create appropriate storage policies for various virtual machines' requirements (for example, for cost-effective and high-performance workloads).

Enabling and creating virtual machine storage policies

Virtual machine storage policies are enabled by default when a VSAN cluster is configured. To manually enable virtual machine storage policies, navigate to the **Home** position on vSphere Web Client, under **Monitoring**, and then select VM **Storage Policies**. Refer to the following screenshot:

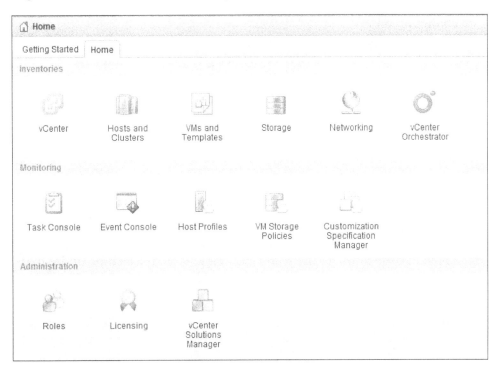

After the virtual machine storage policy has been enabled, the administrator can choose which capability is required from availability and performance perspective, for applications running inside the virtual machine.

The administrator has the flexibility to configure the number of component failures, that is host, networks, and drives; and can also configure the tolerance of the virtual machine for these failures while functioning. Policies can also be configured keeping in view the application requirements of a virtual machine from an IOPS perspective. Also, if required, a flash read cache can be made available or reserved for the said virtual machine to meet its performance requirements.

It is also a common procedure to define multiple levels for virtual machine's performance and availability levels, for example:

- **Bronze**: Cost-effective storage, no flash resources, no resilience
- **Silver**: some flash resources, resilience configuration
- **Gold**: Enhanced I/O performance, high flash resources, enhanced resilience configuration

Assigning a virtual machine storage policy during provisioning

The virtual machine is assigned with a storage policy during its provisioning process. The administrator, when selecting a destination datastore for the virtual machine files, can select an appropriate level of storage policy from the drop-down menu. The datastores are separated into compatible and incompatible datastores, which enables the administrators to choose the correct datastores for virtual machine placement.

To assign a storage policy during virtual machine deployment, perform the following steps:

1. Login to vSphere Web Client and click **New Virtual Machine** under the **Actions** tab.
2. Select **Create a new virtual machine**.
3. Enter a name and select an appropriate location (such as cluster, ESXi host, or folder).
4. Choose a storage policy from **VM Storage Policy**. You will see that all available datastores and datastore clusters are divided into **Compatible** and **Incompatible**.
5. Select a compatible datastore and make changes to DRS, if necessary. Below **Compatibility** you will see whether the chosen datastore is compliant with the selected storage policy.
6. Follow further wizard steps, such as selection of a guest operating system and customizing the virtual machine's hardware configuration.

The following screenshots demonstrates how vSphere Web Client differs between compatible and incompatible datastores:

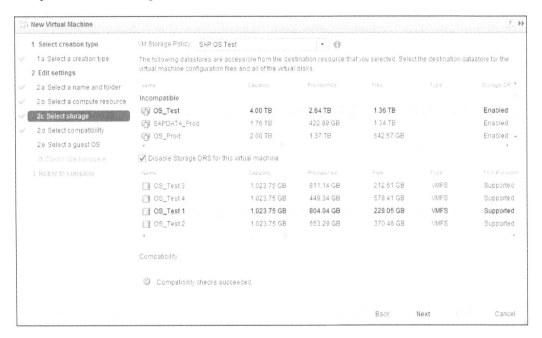

Virtual machine compliance

If the VSAN datastore does not meet the capabilities defined in storage policy, the virtual machine isVSAN: "compliance" said to be noncompliant. If the VSAN meets the capabilities of the storage policy, the virtual machine is in compliant state.

The compliant and the noncompliant status are displayed in the virtual machine's **Summary** tab. To check a virtual machine's compliance status, perform the following steps:

1. Login into vSphere Web Client and select the virtual machine from the inventory.
2. Click **Refresh** on the **VM Storage Policies** pane.

3. Check the status on **VM Storage Policy Compliance**. The following screenshot indicates a virtual machine placed on a compliant datastore:

Failure resilience with VSAN

In this section, we will look at the storage capabilities that can be selected and saved in virtual machine storage policies. These storage capabilities are as follows:

- **Number of failures to tolerate**: This property ensures the availability of the objects by enabling the storage objects to tolerate a defined number of concurrent host, network, or disk failures in the cluster. If this property is populated, it specifies that a virtual machine configuration must withstand at least

  NumberOfFailuresToTolerate + 1 replicas, which may also contain few additional witness objects in order to make sure that the data of the object is available for maintaining quorum un split brain cases, irrespective of that presensce of any NumberOfFailuresToTolerate concurrent host failures; which turns out that we need at least (n+1) replicas of the object and a minimum of (2n + 1) hosts to tolerate n failures.

- **Number of disk stripes per object**: This capability specifies the distribution of replicas of a storage object into the number of physical disks. If the value of this property is higher than 1, it may optimize the performance by utilizing more resources. In case read caching is not effective it will however also result in a greater resource utilization. We need to look into write operations and then move to read operations to understand the impact of disk stripes on storage. All write operations go to the flash device write buffer, which means that the value of an increased disk stripes number might not improve write performance. It doesn't guarantee that the new stripe will use a different Flash-based device, which in turn doesn't improve performance during write operations. The new stripe might be in the same disk group and therefore use the same flash-based device. In case there are multiple write operations to stage from the flash based devices to magnetic discs, then only it is considered to offer advantage in case of write operations. On the other hand, while taking read operations into consideration, an increase in disk stripes numbers improves performance in case of multiple caches misses. Let's assume that a virtual machine is consuming 5,000 read operations per second and is experiencing a cache-hit rate of 90 percent. In such a case, there are 500 read operations per second that need to be serviced from the magnetic disks, which means that a single magnetic disk will not be sufficient for all read operations. Thus, an increase in the disk stripes number would help.

- **Flash read cache reservation**: Flash Read cache reservation refers to the amount of flash memory reserve on any flash based device as a read cache for storage objects. Usually, it is specified as a percentile of the logical size of a VM storage object, and is expressed up to four decimal places of the percentile value. VSAN scheduler allocates fair cache, in case read cache is not reserved for a storage object. Reserved caches can only be accessed by the virtual machines they are reserved for and do not allow any sharing. However, unreserved cache is available for all and is shared among all storage objects fairly.

- **Object space reservation**: Whenever a magnetic disk is initialized, a percentage of the logical size of the storage objects is reserved, which is referred as the object space reservation. VSAN shared datastores are configured with thin provisioning by default. Object space reservation is the amount of space reserved on the VSAN shared datastore, defined in terms of a percentage of the virtual machine disk.

- **Force provisioning**: Force provisioning, when enabled, provisions an object irrespective of the capabilities specified in the virtual machine storage policy, which may or may not be satisfied with the current available resources in the cluster. VSAN attempts to comply with the requirements as and when the resources are available.

Summary

In this chapter, we covered implementation and configuration of VSAN with vSphere. We learnt what VSAN is, and how it is implemented and configured in a vSphere environment. VSAN is not an external appliance but a part of vSphere, and is very scalable as well. It can be enabled/disabled just like HA/DRS cluster. We also learnt how to deploy and change a VM with storage policies and failure resilience with VSAN.

The next chapter will enable us to perform complex advanced operations with virtual machines. It will feature a few of the very important functionalities offered by vSphere such as vMotion, Storage vMotion, and snapshot management.

8
Managing Virtual Machines

In previous chapter, we learnt what Virtual SAN™ (VSAN) is and how it is implemented and configured in a vSphere® environment. VSAN is not an external appliance. It is part of vSphere and is very scalable as well. It is designed as a high-performance and cost-effective hybrid storage. It uses HDD as well as SSD resources, and can be enabled/disabled just like HA/DRS clusters. We also learnt how to deploy and change a VM with storage policies and failure resilience with VSAN.

In *chapter 3, Creating Virtual Machines*, we have already covered virtual machines, templates and how to create templates, how to deploy virtual machine from a template, and how to clone virtual machines. In this chapter, we will discuss the advanced operations that can be performed with virtual machines.

We will cover the following topics:

- Deploying VMs across data centers
- Dynamically updating VM size
- Migrating VMs and templates
- VMware vSphere® vMotion® and VMware vSphere® Storage vMotion®
- VM snapshots

 For ease, we will refer to VMware vSphere® vMotion® as vMotion and VMware vSphere® Storage vMotion® as Storage vMotion in this chapter.

Deploying virtual machines across data centers

vCenter allows the administrator to provision virtual machines across the virtual data centers that are managed by the same vCenter Server instance. Virtual machine deployment is allowed across data centers. The administrator can:

- Clone a virtual machine from one virtual data center to another virtual data center

- Create a template in one data center, deploy a virtual machine from that template, and place the virtual machine in another virtual data center

> We already covered deploying virtual machines in *chapter 3, Creating Virtual Machines*.

Modifying the virtual machine settings

The administrator might have to change a virtual machine configuration, for example adding another virtual hard disk or adding another network adapter. The administrator can change all virtual machine settings while the virtual machine is powered off. However, some hardware changes can be made to the virtual machine even while the virtual machine is running, such as adding hard disks. The dialog also gives the administrator the possibility to remove virtual hardware and set options such as controlling the virtual machine's CPU and memory.

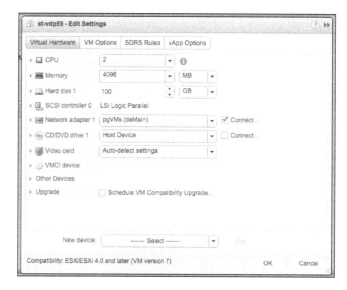

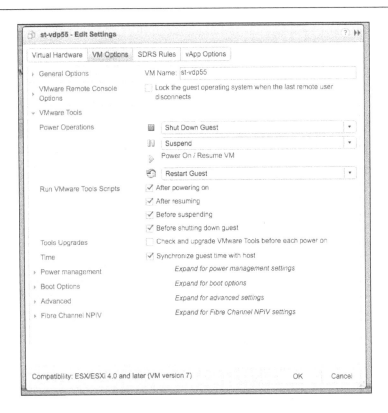

The entire virtual machine configuration can be changed using the virtual machine's **Edit Settings** dialog box. To display virtual machine's properties, right-click the virtual machine in the inventory and click **Edit Settings**. You can use the **Virtual Hardware** tab to modify the virtual hardware of the virtual machine. It is also possible to use the legacy vSphere client for altering a virtual machine's configuration. However, as it is not supported to configure the most recent virtual hardware features (introduced in VMHW 8 or higher), administrators should prefer vSphere Web Client.

Adding devices to a virtual machine

Adding or removing devices to physical server requires administrator to physically interact with the server in the data center. When using virtual machine, resources can be added or removed dynamically with zero loss in service. The administrator might need to shut down the virtual machine to remove virtual hardware, but he can reconfigure the virtual machine without being physically present at the data center.

To add a virtual hardware to a virtual machine, follow the next steps:

1. Right-click the virtual machine and select **Edit Settings**.
2. Select the **Virtual Hardware** tab in the **Edit Settings** dialog box.
3. In the new device drop-down menu, select the hardware which you would like to add and click on **Add**.

The following screenshot shows some of the hardware that can be added to a virtual machine:

CPU and memory can also be added while the virtual machine is powered on. This feature is known as **CPU Hot-Plug** and **Memory Hot-Add** option. To use these features:

*   VMware tools must be installed on the virtual machine
*   Virtual machine must use hardware version 7 or later
*   The guest operating system must support the CPU hot-plug and memory hot-add features
*   The hot plug option must be enabled in VM options tab under the **Edit Settings** dialog box

Increasing the size of a virtual disk

The administrator can increase the size of a virtual disk attached to a virtual machine, while the virtual machine is powered on. Virtual machine disk size can be increased if the virtual machine is a flat virtual disk in persistent mode and virtual machine doesn't have any snapshots. If the virtual hard disk is provisioned in Thick-Provision Eager-Zeroed mode, it will automatically become Thick-Provision Lazy-Zeroed after expanding the size. You can convert it back by migrating the appropriate disk using Storage vMotion, while specifying the Eager-Zeroed allocation mode.

To increase the size of a virtual disk, perform the following steps:

1. Login into vCenter Server using vSphere Web Client.

2. Right-click the virtual machine in the inventory and select **Edit settings**.

3. Select the hard disk in the hardware list.

4. Type the new size of the hard disk.

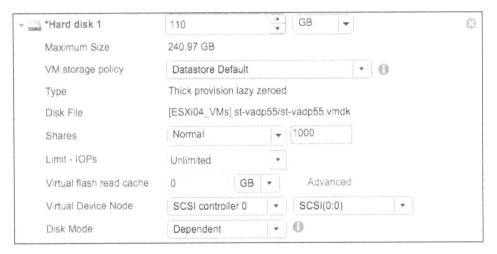

After the size of the disk is increased, the administrator must increase the size of the file system on this disk. The administrator should use the appropriate tool inside the guest operating system to enable the file system to use newly allocated disk space. For example, if administrator is using Windows 2003 or XP, he can use the **disk part** utility to increase the file system on the disk. For Windows 2008 and 7 onwards, these operating systems have inbuilt tools to expand the file system. For Linux systems, there are plenty tools available depending on the used file system such as **resize2fs** and **xfs_growfs**.

Inflating a thin provisioned disk

The administrator can inflate a thin provisioned disk; the inflated virtual disk occupies the entire datastore space originally provisioned to it. Inflating a Thin-provisioned disk converts a thin disk in a Thick-Provision format.

To inflate a thin provisioned disk, perform the following steps:

1. Login using vSphere Web Client.
2. Select the virtual machine from the inventory and click **Edit Settings**.
3. Expand the virtual disk you want to inflate. Note that the **Disk File** field contains the datastore path to the virtual disk.
4. Cancel the wizard and select the appropriate datastore path by selecting **Related Objects** and **Datastores**.
5. Navigate to the path you discovered in the wizard.
6. Right-click the VMDK file and select **Inflate**.

 A more user-friendly way to convert Thin-provisioned disks into Thick-Provision format is to use Storage vMotion. We will cover this in the next section.

Migrating virtual machines

Migration is the process of moving a virtual machine from one host or datastore to another host or datastore. Migrating virtual machines applies to multiple possible use cases including:

- Preparing an ESXi host or storage unit for maintenance to avoid virtual machine downtime
- Balancing load between ESXi hosts
- Freeing up space on particular datastores

There are seven types of migration that can be performed on virtual machines, which are:

- **Cold migration**: Cold migration refers to moving a virtual machine that is powered off. In cold migration, the administrator can change the host, datastore, or both. Cold migration is supported across virtual data centers, which means that the administrator can move a virtual machine from one virtual data center to another. For cold migration, shared storage is not required.

- **Suspended migration**: This means migration of a virtual machine that is in suspended state. In suspended migration also, the administrator can change the host, datastore, or both, and it is supported across virtual data centers too. This means that the administrator can move a virtual machine from one virtual data center to another. Also, shared storage is not required here as well.

- **vMotion**: This is a process of migrating a virtual machine that is powered on. In vMotion, the administrator can only change the host of the virtual machine, and it is not supported across data centers. In addition, it requires a shared storage.

- **Storage vMotion**: This enables migrating a virtual machine files while the virtual machine is powered on to another datastore. The administrator can only change the datastore and has no control over the host. Storage vMotion is not supported across data centers and shared storage is not required.

- **Enhanced vMotion**: This is a process of migrating a virtual machine from one host to another, and virtual machine files from one datastore to another simultaneously, while the virtual machine is running. It is a combination of vMotion and Storage vMotion. It is not supported across data centers and does not require any kind of shared storage. Enhanced vMotion is only supported using vSphere Web Client.

- **Long-distance vMotion**: Beginning with vSphere 6.0, vMotion is also supported on network connections with up to 100ms **Round Trip Time (RTT)** latency; previously the limitation was 10ms RTT. Using this, it is possible to migrate workloads between metro-clusters and continents.

- **Cross-vCenter / Cross-vSwitch vMotion**: Another feature that came with vSphere 6.0 is Cross-vCenter / Cross-vSwitch vMotion. Using this, the administrator is able to migrate workloads between multiple vCenter Server installations. It is possible to change compute, storage or networking resources during the migration, but it is not possible to switch from vNetwork standard to distributed virtual switch, or vice versa. When migrating between vCenter installations, it is required that both installations are part of the same **Single-Sign On (SSO)** domain. As this is also supported between vCenter Server and vCenter Server Appliance, it makes infrastructure migrations much easier.

Using VMware vMotion

VMware vMotion migrates a powered on virtual machine from one ESXi host to another without any downtime. vMotion is the backbone of vSphere **Distributed Resource Scheduler** (**DRS**), which uses vMotion to migrate virtual machines from one host to another and balances the load. With vSphere vMotion, the entire state of the virtual machine is moved from one host to another while the data on the storage remains on the same datastore. The state information consists of the current memory contents of the virtual machine, and all the information that is specific to the virtual machine apart from the memory are bios, hardware devices, CPU, and MAC address for the ethernet cards. Following are the steps for vMotion migrations:

1. The virtual memory state is copied from the source ESXi to target ESXi over the vMotion network. The list of modified pages in memory is kept in the memory bitmap on the source host.

2. After the memory has been copied from source to destination ESXi host, no additional activity can occur on the virtual machine.

3. In this state, vMotion transfers the virtual machine device state and memory bitmap to the destination host.

4. Immediately after the virtual machine goes into a halt or quiesce state, the virtual machine is initialized and starts running on the target host.

5. Users can now access the virtual machine on the target host instead of the source host.

6. Memory pages that the virtual machine was using on the source host are marked as free.

Use cases for vMotion include:

*   **Maintenance tasks without downtime**: If one ESXi host in a cluster needs hardware maintenance, such as replacing spare parts, virtual machines can be moved to another node to ensure VM availability. As a result, end-users won't notice that maintenance tasks are being processed.

*   **Load-balancing**: When running a cluster, vMotion can be used to balance CPU and memory consumption between particular ESXi hosts to enable a fair use of resources. Using DRS and Storage DRS, this is done automatically by executing vMotion and Storage vMotion.

*   **Application resilience**: Clustered applications running inside multiple virtual machines can be distributed on multiple ESXi hosts, to ensure availability in case of a faulty ESXi host. In combination with DRS groups and VM-host affinity rules, it is possible to ensure that particular virtual machines are always placed separately on different ESXi hosts.

Virtual machine requirements for vMotion

vMotion depends on a lot of conditions that need to be fulfilled. Let us look at the virtual machine requirements for vMotion:

- A virtual machine must not have a connection to an internal only standard virtual switch; that is a virtual switch which doesn't have an uplink connected to it

- A virtual machine must not have a connection to CD/DVD image mounted locally

- A virtual machine should not have CPU affinity rules configured

- If the virtual machine swap file is on a different datastore, which is not accessible from the destination, then vMotion must be able to create a swap file that is accessible to the destination before the migration can begin

- If a virtual machine has a connection to RDM, then that RDM must be accessible from the destination host as well

Host requirements for vMotion

The source and the destination hosts must have the following characteristics:

- Visibility to all kinds of storage used by virtual machines (iSCSI Fiber channel or NAS)

- At least 1 Gigabit Ethernet connectivity

- Port group names should be same across source and destination hosts (if Cross-vSwitch vMotion is not available)

- The host should have compatible CPUs. To also enable migrating workloads between different processor generations or vendors, it is required to enable VMware **Enhanced vMotion Compatibility** (**EVC**)

VMware Enhanced vMotion Compatibility (EVC)

By default, vMotion operations are only supported between equal processor generations and vendors. This feature can be useful if an ESXi cluster consists of hosts with differing hardware configurations (for example, added spare hosts to reduce costs). Using EVC can also be very useful when migrating workloads to a new virtual infrastructure without shutting down the particular virtual machines. If enabled, all hosts are configured to provide the same set of CPU functions. In other words, functions of newer CPU generations are disabled for ESXi to match those of older hosts in the cluster. It is not supported to migrate workloads between Intel and AMD based hosts. The only way to migrate VMs between Intel and AMD based hosts is Cold migration.

EVC is enabled at cluster level, specifying a particular EVC mode. This mode defines which CPU generation is used as EVC baseline. Once enabled, all hosts will be configured to mask out CPU functions not defined in the selected EVC baseline. Masking out particular functions means that they are not exposed to virtual machines. The EVC baseline needs to be set to the lowest function set that all ESXi host's CPUs support (the oldest host in the cluster). Selecting the most recent EVC baselines is only supported using vSphere Web Client.

EVC requirements

Make sure to fulfill the following requirements before enabling EVC:

- Make sure that your CPU generation is supported along with your vCenter Server version. This can be checked at `http://kb.vmware.com/kb/1003212`. Also, verify that your CPU generation is basically supported for your ESXi release. This can be verified at `http://www.vmware.com/resources/compatibility/search.php?deviceCategory=cpu`.

- All ESXi hosts must either have only Intel or AMD CPUs. It is not supported to mix vendors.

- Hardware virtualization bits (Intel VT or AMD-V) must be enabled on all the nodes.

- vMotion networking needs to be configured equally on all the hosts.

Configuring EVC

To enable EVC, perform the following steps:

1. Login to vCenter Server using vSphere Web Client.
2. Select the affected cluster from the inventory.
3. Right-click and click **Manage**, **Settings**, **VMware EVC**, and **Edit**.
4. Choose between **Enable EVC for AMD Hosts** and **Enable EVC for Intel®** **Hosts**. Also select the appropriate CPU generation for the cluster.
5. Ensure that **Compatibility** acknowledges your configuration, before saving the changes.

Configuration of EVC can also be done during cluster creation.

Migrating a virtual machine

To migrate a virtual machine, which meets the requirements mentioned in the previous sections from source to destination, proceed with the following steps:

1. Login to vCenter Server using vSphere Web Client.

2. Select the virtual machine from the inventory.

3. Right-click the powered on virtual machine and select **Migrate**.

4. In the **Migrate** wizard, select **Change Host** option to perform vMotion.

5. Select an appropriate host; a validation check is performed to verify the vMotion requirements have been met or not.

6. If the validation succeeds, then the administrator can continue in the wizard; if not, list of vMotion errors are displayed in the compatibility pane. If any failure occurs during the vMotion migration, the virtual machine which was being migrated fails back to the source host.

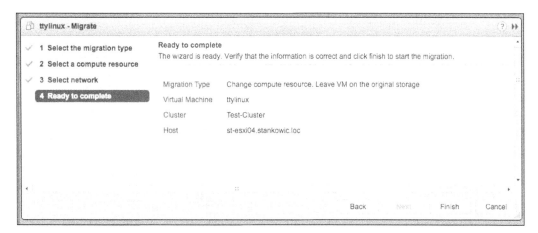

Alternatively, to migrate workloads, you can also drag and drop virtual machines to other ESXi hosts in the inventory list. This will automatically open the vMotion wizard.

Using Storage vMotion

vSphere Storage vMotion is a feature of vSphere that enables the administrator to migrate the virtual machine disk files from one datastore to another datastore, while the virtual machine is powered on.

The following are some use cases for Storage vMotion:

- **Simplifying storage array migration and storage upgrades**: The administrator can migrate the virtual machines from source datastore to destination datastore, and take advantages such as flexible leasing models, retiring old storage, or conducting storage upgrades.

- **Dynamically optimizing the storage IO performance**: The administrator can move the virtual machine to an alternate datastore that can provide optimal performance which the virtual machine needs, without any downtime.

- **Efficiently managing storage capacity:** The administrator can distribute the virtual disk files of the virtual machine across all datastores, to effectively manage their capacity.

Migrating a virtual machine using Storage vMotion

To accomplish Storage vMotion in your virtual environment, proceed with the following steps:

1. Right-click the powered on virtual machine and select **Migrate**.

2. In **Migrate** wizard, select **Change storage only**.

3. Select a datastore and make sure that **Compatibility** acknowledges your selection.

Guidelines to use Storage vMotion

Storage vMotion needs to follow a certain set of guidelines while it's being processed, in order to smoothly and successfully complete the migration. Following are the guidelines to consider:

- Storage vMotion should be performed during off peak hours.

- Ensure that the ESXi host has access to both source and destination datastores.

- Files moved by Storage vMotion will automatically be renamed at the destination. It is a common practice to run Storage vMotion after renaming a virtual machine's name to also rename datastore folder names.

vSphere Storage vMotion has the limitation that the virtual machine disks must be in persistent mode or be RDMs in order for the migration to be completed.

Using Enhanced vMotion

Enhanced vMotion enables the administrator to change a virtual machine's host and the datastore simultaneously, when the virtual machine is powered on, even if the source and the datastore hosts do not have a shared storage in common.

Enhanced vMotion can only be performed through the vSphere Web Client. Using the vSphere legacy client along with Enhanced vMotion is not supported.

Host requirements for Enhanced vMotion

Enhanced vMotion is a single migration to change both hosts and datastores. The following requirements need to be met:

- Hosts must be managed by the same vCenter Server instance
- Hosts must be part of the same virtual data center
- Hosts must be on the same layer 2 network

The following are the optional considerations for Enhanced vMotion:

- Enhanced vMotion is a manual process. DRS and storage DRS cannot leverage Enhanced vMotion
- Maximum of 2 concurrent Enhanced vMotion migrations are possible on an ESXi host
- Enhanced vMotion leverages multiple NICs whenever available

Migrating a virtual machine using Enhanced vMotion

To migrate a virtual machine by using Enhanced vMotion, proceed with the following steps:

1. Right-click the powered on virtual machine and select **Migrate**.
2. In the **Migrate** wizard, select **Change both compute resource and storage**.
3. Select a computing resource such as a cluster or a particular ESXi host. Make sure that compatibility checks succeed before clicking **Next**.
4. Select a new datastore. You can also specify a new disk provisioning format and storage policy.

5. Select a new port group if you want to change network options.

6. By default, the migration process is started with high priorization. If the ESXi host is on high CPU usage, it is also possible to schedule a lower CPU priorization; in such a case, the migration will take more time.

Virtual machine snapshots

Snapshot enables the administrator to preserve the state of the virtual machine so that it can be returned to the same state repeatedly. For example, if the administrator does some patching or upgrading of the operating system of the virtual machine, snapshots give him the ability to withdraw those changes if any problem occurs during the operation.

Snapshot preserves both the state of virtual machine and data at a specific point in time. State refers to the virtual machine's powered state, which can be powered on, powered off, or suspended. Data includes the files that make up the virtual machine, including the disks, memory, and other virtual hardware devices like NICs. It is important to understand that snapshots should not be used for backup purposes, as the virtual machine size can increase drastically. Once a snapshot is created, all changes to virtual disks are stored in delta files. As a result, a virtual machine might consume the doubled size on storage if every bit is changed on its virtual disks. If multiple snapshots are created, the most recent snapshot refers to the previous snapshot, also resulting in doubled size. It is advisable to delete snapshots as fast as possible, as the virtual machine's I/O performance also suffers from the created snapshots.

A virtual machine can have one or more than one snapshots. Each snapshot consists of the following set of files:

- **Memory state file** (`vmname-snapshot#.vmsn`): This file holds the memory state at the time the snapshot was taken. While taking the snapshot, if the administrator captures the memory, the size of this file is equal to the maximum size of the memory of that virtual machine. If the machine's memory is not captured, the file size is much smaller.

- **Disk descriptor file** (`vmname-0000#.vmdk`): This file is a text file that describes the snapshot and contains relevant information about it.

- **Snapshot delta file** (`vmname-0000#-delta.vmdk`): This file contains the changes to the virtual disk's data when the snapshot was taken.

- **Snapshot list file** (`vmname.vmsd`): This is the snapshot list file created when the virtual machine is created. It maintains the snapshot information so that it can create a list of snapshots in the vSphere Web Client.

The process of taking snapshots

To take a snapshot, proceed with the following steps:

1. To take a snapshot, right-click the virtual machine in the inventory and select **Snapshots** and **Take snapshot**.

2. In the **Take VM Snapshot** dialog box, a **Name** and **Description** for the snapshot (for example, snapshot before OS patches).

3. If you want to have the guest operating system's memory content included in the snapshot, check **Snapshot the virtual machine's memory**. If disabled, the virtual machine will be in powered off state if the snapshot is reverted to.

4. If VMware Tools are installed in the guest operating system, it is possible to initialize file system synchronization before creating the snapshot. As a result, all content cached in the file system is written to disk, to ensure that the snapshot contains all relevant changes. To enable this feature, check **Quiesce guest file system**.

The administrator can take the snapshot when the machine is on, off, or suspended. Integrating virtual machine memory and quiescing the guest file system is only available while the virtual machine is running.

Managing snapshots

Right-click the virtual machine in the inventory, select snapshot, and click on **Snapshot Manager**.

In **Snapshot Manager**, the administrator can do the following tasks:

- **Delete**: This carries out the task of merging the snapshot data with the parent snapshot, and then removes the selected snapshot.

- **Delete all**: It merges all the immediate snapshots before the current state and removes all the snapshots.

- **Revert to**: This enables the administrator to restore or revert back to a particular snapshot. The snapshot that the administrator reverts to becomes the current snapshot.

Summary

In this chapter, we have learnt about advanced operations that can be performed with virtual machines such as deployment, updating sizes, and migration of virtual machines and templates using vMotion. We also learnt about the requirements and processes of storage vMotion and Enhanced vMotion. We also understood the purpose and usage of virtual machine snapshots.

In the next chapter, we will have a deeper look at resource management and performance monitoring. Especially, we will learn about memory commitment and resource pools. We will also learn how to implement and manage events and alarms.

9

Resource Management and Performance Monitoring

In previous chapter, we looked at advanced operations that can be performed with virtual machines like deployment across data centers, updating sizes, and migration of virtual machines and templates using vMotion, Storage vMotion, and Enhanced vMotion. We also covered virtual machine snapshots.

This chapter focuses on how to efficiently manage resources on the server. We will learn how to effectively manage available resources and also learn of ways to monitor their performance. We will start by learning about managing the virtual memory on the server, and then proceed to understand resource pools and controls. All resources need to be allocated with strategy, hence we will be learning how to implement shares, limitations, and reservations on resources. This chapter also talks about how to monitor resource usage so that the administrator is aware if the resources are being utilized properly. We will also learn about how to implement alarms to notify the administrator in case of failing resources.

Following is the list of topics we will cover:

- Virtual memory management
- Understanding resource controls and resource pools
- Implementing shares, limits, and reservations on resources
- Monitoring resource usage
- Alarms and notifications

Although VMkernel is working proactively to avoid resource contention, the administrator should know the options which are available to maximize the performance, and monitor the resource utilization of the virtual machine and the ESXi host.

Virtual memory management

Virtual memory refers to the memory available for virtual machines from the physical memory present on the host. VMkernel makes the operating system in a virtual machine take the virtual memory and use it as a physical memory for all its operations. Virtual memory is not limited to the size of the physical memory available, and can be extended or limited as per requirements of the virtual machine.

vSphere offers flexible memory management solutions and different kind of memories as per different needs. Three different memories used by vSphere are:

- **Host physical memory**: The memory which is physically present on the host. This memory is managed by VMkernel and provides addressable memory space to the virtual machine.

- **Guest operating system physical memory**: The memory which is presented to the virtual machine once it is created.

- **Guest operating system virtual memory**: The memory which is presented to the application by the guest operating system.

Virtual machine memory over-commitment

Memory over commitment occurs when the physical memory installed on the physical ESXi host is less than the sum of the memory allocated to the virtual machines on that host. When an ESXi host memory is over committed, VMkernel uses several techniques for virtual machines to utilize the memory. In this section, we will talk about these few techniques. Basically, it is preferable to avoid memory over commitment to ensure that all virtual machines can address the memory resources they need.

Virtual machine swap files

Virtual machine swap files are created when a virtual machine is powered on. The size of the virtual machine's swap file is equal to the size of the allocated memory minus its reservation (you will know more about reservation in the *Understanding resource controls and resource pools* section).

Memory reclamation techniques

VMware uses various techniques to reclaim memory assigned to ESXi hosts.
These are:

- **Transparent page sharing**: TPS allows pages with identical content to be stored only once. So if there are multiple virtual machines with identical pages (for example, in Virtual Desktop Infrastructure setups), TPS will only store them once in the memory, and hence allow higher level of memory commitment. In December 2014/January 2015, VMware decided to disable this feature between particular virtual machines by default because of independent research studies regarding TPS. Those results demonstrated that it might be possible to gain access to shared memory resources. To address this, VMware also implemented a more secure memory salting mechanism. Administrators are able to enable Intra-VM TPS as per their needs. Details can be found on the VMware knowledge base at `http://kb.vmware.com/kb/2080735`.

- **Ballooning**: During the times of memory contention, VMkernel looks for the opportunity to reclaim idle and unallocated memory from virtual machines, and transfer that to some other virtual machines that need more memory. Ballooning happens using the VMware memory control driver (VMMEMCTL) that is installed with VMware tools. The VMMEMCTL driver is also called the balloon driver.

- **Memory Compression**: Memory compression is another technique which VMkernel uses to reclaim host physical memory. This technique attempts to reclaim some memory by compressing memory pages. Using this mechanism produces a negligible amount of overhead, but it is still more effective than paging memory to disk.

- **Host Level SSD swapping**: This option will be used after TPS, ballooning, and memory compression have been tried. In this option, the administrator can configure a SSD as a host cache. This host cache will be used as a swap space for the virtual machine.

- **Page virtual machine memory out to disk**: This is the last and the least desirable technique in which the virtual machine memory is moved out to the disk. The performance is very poor when this technique is used. Basically, the administrator should size ESXi hosts so that this technique is not used during normal operation.

Virtual CPU

An administrator can configure a virtual machine with as many as 128 vCPUs on vSphere 6.0 (vSphere 5.5: 64). The VMkernel scheduler dynamically schedules vCPUs on the physical CPU of the server. A vCPU is the central processing unit of the v2ioirtual machine. When a vCPU of a single or multi vCPU virtual machine has to be scheduled, VMkernel maps the vCPU to available logical processor.

CPU load balancing

The CPU scheduler can use each logical processor individually to map it to virtual machines. VMkernel manages the processor time to guarantee that the load is distributed across all the cores in the system. Every two to 40 miliseconds, VMkernel looks to migrate the vCPU from one logical processor to another, to keep the load fairly balanced.

VKkernel does the best to schedule virtual machines on different cores rather than have two logical processors on the same core.

Hyper-threading

Hyper-threading gives the ability to a core to execute to threads or two sets of instructions simultaneously. Hyper-threading, when enabled, can increase the performance of the CPU. Beginning with vSphere 5.x, VMware highly recommends enabling Hyper-threading on ESXi hosts. To enable Hyper-threading, the following steps need to be performed:

1. Check if your system supports Hyper-threading. Check your vendor's manual and CPU datasheet regarding this.

2. Enable Hyper-threading in the system's BIOS settings.

3. Login into vCenter Server using vSphere Web Client.

4. Select the host from the inventory.

5. Click **Manage**, **Settings**, and select **Advanced System Settings** under **System**. To turn on Hyper-threading, set the value for the setting **VMkernel. Boot.hyperthreading** to **true**.

Understanding resource controls and resource pools

As multiple virtual machines run on the same ESXi host simultaneously, vSphere has a lot of mechanisms for proper resource management.

Resource controls

To start with resource management, it is sufficient to understand the concept of resource controls. There are three configurable parameters to control virtual machine's access to a given resource. These are:

- **Shares**: Shares specify the relative priority or importance of a virtual machine's access to a given resource in case of resource contention.
- **Limits**: This is the maximum amount of CPU or memory that can be consumed by a virtual machine.
- **Reservation**: This is the minimum amount of CPU or memory that is guaranteed to a particular virtual machine. The virtual machine will not power on if its reservations are not met, to avoid poor performance.

Resource pools

A resource pool is a logical abstraction for hierarchically managing CPU and memory resources. It can be used on a standalone host or can be created on a cluster as well. Resource pools provide resources for virtual machines and child resource pools, including:

- CPU (including advanced settings such as Hyper-threading modes and CPU affinity rules)
- Memory
- Disk

A resource pool allows the administrator to divide and allocate resources to virtual machines and other child resource pools. The first resource pool is called a root resource pool. The root resource pool does not appear, because the resources of the host (or cluster) and root resource pool are always the same.

Following are the benefits of using resource pools:

- Flexible hierarchical organization
- Isolation between resource pools
- Access control delegation
- Separation of resources from hardware
- Management of sets of virtual machines

For a better understanding, let's start with an easy example. Let's say, a company uses an ESXi host with production and development workloads. As production virtual machines are mission-critical, development virtual machines should not exceed defined limits.

To address these requirements, a solution would be to create two resource pools with reservations and limitations. Refer to the following image:

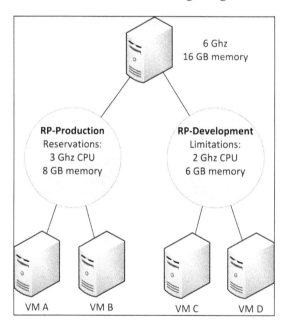

Creating a resource pool

The administrator can create a resource pool on a stand-alone ESXi host, on a cluster level, or in another resource pool.

To create a resource pool, perform the following steps:

1. Login into vCenter Server using the vSphere Web Client.
2. Right-click the host, a cluster, or a resource pool.
3. Select all vCenter actions.
4. Click on **New resource pool**.
5. The create resource pool dialog will pop up. Similar to virtual machines, a resource pool also has shares, limits, and reservations for CPUs and memory.

> vSphere DRS must be enabled to configure and utilize resource pools.

Expandable reservation

Expandable reservation is an attribute that is specific to a resource pool. This attribute allows a resource pool that is not able to satisfy the reservation request for a particular machine and search through its parent for unreserved capacity to satisfy the reservation request.

The administrator should use the expandable reservation carefully; a child resource pool can use all of its parent's available resources, leaving nothing directly available for other child resource pools.

The administrator can use the resource pool summary tab to display information that applies to the host machine and its resources. The **Resource Settings** pane displays CPU and memory share settings, and the **Resource Consumers** pane displays the number of virtual machines, number of powered on virtual machines, and number of child resource pools that are in the selected resource pool.

The **Tags** pane shows tags assigned to the object in this particular resource pool. The **Commands** pane allows the administrator to create resource pool and edit its settings. The following screenshot demonstrates vSphere Web Client displaying a resource pool's settings and consumption:

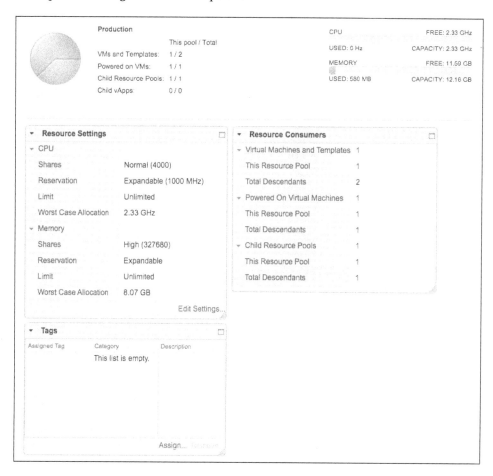

The resource utilization tab allows the administrator to display information about the resource pool's hardware including CPU, memory, and storage resources. To view this tab click **Monitor** and **Utilization**.

The following information is displayed under the **Resource allocation** tab:

- Amount of CPU and memory reservation configured
- The type of reservation used
- Amount of reservation used by virtual machines used in child pools
- Amount of CPU and memory available

The screenshot below shows a resource pool's CPU and memory reservations, shares, limits and consumption:

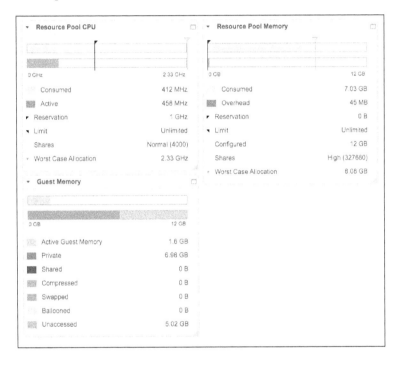

Implementing shares, limits, and reservations on resource pools

Shares, limits, and reservation settings can be viewed under the **Manage** tab of every virtual machine, and can be configured individually for every resource. The following image shows shares, limits and reservations of a particular virtual machine:

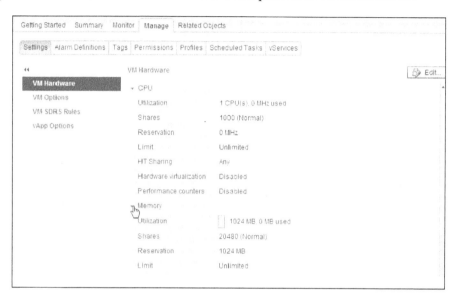

To modify the settings or configure the shares, limits, and reservations on any of the resource, click on the **Edit** button on the VM hardware section, and under the **Edit Settings** page, select the desired configuration for every resource. For example, the following screenshot illustrates modification of share allocation for a vCPU for a VM:

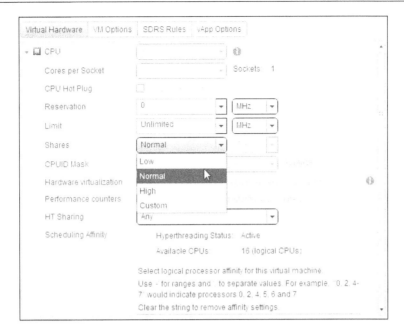

When a host memory or CPU is over-committed, a virtual machine's allocation target is somewhere between its specified reservation and specified limit, depending on the virtual machine's shares and the system load.

To implement a reservation, for example, to reserve a physical memory of 1 GB for a virtual machine, under the **Edit Settings** dialog box, change the memory size in **Reservations** pane as shown in the following image:

Similarly, we can also limit the utilization of resources of virtual machines which need not use a lot of resources such as test machines or development environment. To control the utilization of resources in such cases, we use the limits to specify the maximum resource utilization allowed. For example, for a test machine, maximum CPU resource available is 4000 Mhz. We can limit it, as shown in the following image, and it can be performed the same way for memory, storage, network, and so on:

Monitoring resource usage

All resources in a virtual environment can be centrally monitored for over utilization and performance reports. Four of the most critical resources to be monitored are CPU, memory, storage disks, and network. To monitor these resources, VMware offers a wide array of applications, which can be used from inside the guest operating system, or via vCenter Web Client or the legacy vSphere client. There are also third-party applications to monitor resources. However, the best approach towards monitoring resources and ensuring their maximum and efficient utilization, is by performance tuning the resources.

Performance tuning is more art than science and needs customization as per requirements. However, the logical approach involves a four-step process in order to attain the best outcome. Following are these steps:

1. To control the performance of resources, make sure to use resource-monitoring tools both at operating system and vCenter Server level.

2. Identify the most important resources for individual virtual machines. If they are unavailable the operating capabilities or performance of the virtual machine might hamper.

3. Also check other virtual machine's to ensure that they are consuming only the resources they need. Make sure not to waste unneeded resources, they could be useful for other workloads.

4. Record changes from step one; that is, before implementing of the monitoring tools and then after performance tuning the data center.

These changes may hamper performance of virtual machines as well, if not configured properly. Hence, it is advisable to make sure all the virtual machines are working properly after changes, and have enough resources available for smooth operations.

Now that we know that the first step of performance tuning is installing monitoring tools, let's talk about a few resource-monitoring tools available for VMware architecture:

- **Guest operating system**: Tools such as perfmon.dll, IOmeter, and even Windows Task Manager can be used to monitor resource utilization inside virtual machines. For UNIX or Linux hosts, there are plenty of platform-dependent tools including **top**, **ps**, **free**, **vmstat**, and **sar**. Perfmon, being part of VMware tools, enables the administrator to access host statistics in the guest operating system.

- **vCenter Server performance charts**: vCenter Server offers a great performance chart engine which serves plenty of metrics based on gathered information inside the virtual environment. vCenter Server collects resource information such as CPU, memory, network and storage utilization.

- **vRealize Operations**: This suite, which was formerly called vCenter Operations Manager, offers a broad range of features for intelligent resource management. It offers customizable dashboards, and helps with capacity monitoring and future planning (what-if analysis). For example, it can assist you with determining wasted resources and also role-based security rules. Seamlessly integrated with vSphere and other virtual infrastructures such as Microsoft Hyper-V and **Amazon Web Services** (**AWS**), it can also be used for hybrid infrastructure scenarios. vRealize Operations collects information about the norm state of the infrastructure; as a result, the tool is able to detect anomalies and inform the administrator before a fault arises. The product is available in three editions (Standard, Advanced, and Enterprise), offering different feature sets for customers' needs.

- **vRealize Log Insight**: This utility (formerly vCenter Log Insight) offers centralized log collection and management functionality for all components of virtual infrastructures including network, application, vSphere, guest operating system, and applications. As all the information is collected centrally, customers are able to perform detailed log analysis. The utility is also optimized for physical and cloud setups; it is often used along with vRealize Operations.

- **esxtop/resxtop**: **esxtop** is a very handy utility for performance and resource monitoring on ESXi hosts. It offers many metrics for CPU, memory, network, and storage. **resxtop** is a vSphere CLI command that can be used to gather information from a remote ESXi host on Windows and Linux systems.

Alarms and notifications

An alarm is a notification that is triggered as a result of a condition that was pre-configured for an object in the virtual infrastructure. There are default alarms in the vSphere environment, and a user can also create custom alarms as per requirements and criticality of a particular resource. Alarms can be set for all objects in the infrastructure inventory such as virtual machines, data centers, datastores, clusters, hosts, switches, port groups, network, and so on.

All predefined or default alarms can also be modified to meet the needs of the current infrastructure. The custom alarms are created if the requirements are not met by editing or modifying the existing alarms to monitor the desired resource.

To look at some alarms, which are triggered by default, first go to Event Console under the Monitoring section in vSphere Web Client. In the **Event Console**, you will see **Cautions** and **Warnings**, highlighted in red and yellow colors.

An alarm for an object can be viewed by selecting the object. Under the **Manage** tab, go to the option **Alarm definitions**. Additional alarms can be created from there as well. However the generic method to create an alarm is as follows:

1. Right-click on the object in the inventory.
2. Select **Alarm** and then the **Add Alarm** option.
3. The **New Alarm Definition** dialog box will appear; furnish the alarm details, and its triggers and actions.
4. Select the check box **Enable this alarm**.

The following figure shows the alarm wizard in vSphere Web Client:

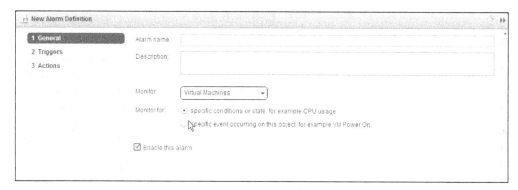

An alarm can be triggered on any of the two monitoring aspects, that is condition triggers or event triggers. Condition triggers are used to monitor condition or state of the inventory objects such as power state of a virtual machine, connection state of a storage cluster, and so on. On the other hand, event triggers are used to monitor events that occur in context to any operation or function performed by any object, such as deletion, migration, or creation of a virtual machine in a data center.

Let's have a look at a useful example. We will configure a alarm for virtual machines having snapshots. The following procedure demonstrates how to generate alarms once virtual machine snapshots are created. As a result, snapshots are visible in the alarm section of vSphere Web Client; we can also send notifications using e-mails.

1. Login to vCenter Server using vSphere Web Client.

2. Select your vCenter or another entity such as a folder, a cluster, or a particular ESXi host from the inventory. The alarm will be created at the selected level.

3. Click on **Manage**, **Alarm Definitions** and the **Add** icon.

4. Enter an **Alarm name** and **Description** (for example, Snapshot, Generates an alarm once a VM snapshot is created).

5. For **Monitor**, select **Virtual Machines**. Also, select **Monitor for specific conditions or state, for example CPU usage**. Make sure to check **Enable this alarm**.

   The following screenshot shows the alarm creation wizard with entered values:

6. Click the **Add** icon and select **VM Snapshot Size** from the drop-down list.

7. Select **operator is above** and set warning and critical thresholds (for example, 1 GB warning and 10 GB critical). Proceed to the next step.

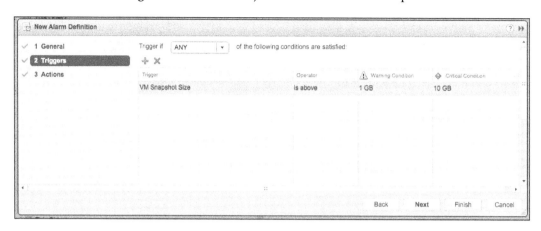

8. Click the **Add** icon again to assign a trigger to be executed once an alarm is generated. The default is **Send a notification email**; in the **Configuration** column, a mail address needs to be entered.

9. Specify how often mails should be sent. It is possible to execute triggers once or on repetition until a status change is recognized. Configurable status changes include **From normal to warning**, **From warning to critical**, **From critical to warning**, and **From warning to normal**. In our example, it would be possible to repeat sending mails until a virtual machine's snapshot is removed. The administrator can specify how often action triggers should be repeated; the default is 5 minutes.

10. Click **Finish** to create the alarm.

Summary

In this chapter, we covered how to manage and monitor resources on the virtual infrastructure, and how to achieve their maximum utilization. We now know how to effectively manage available resources and ways to monitor their performance. This chapter also made us aware about how to monitor resource usage, so that the administrator is aware if the resources are utilized properly or not. In case of failing resources, we also know how to implement and control alarms to inform the administrator.

In the next chapter, we will have a look at High Availability and Fault Tolerance. Especially, we will learn how to implement and control these techniques to ensure availability in case of failures. We will also cover the configuration of DRS and Storage DRS to enable automatic workload and resource load-balancing.

10
Incorporating vSphere High Availability, Fault Tolerance, and DRS

In the previous chapter, we learnt how to manage and monitor resources on the virtual infrastructure, and how to achieve their maximum utilization. We now know how to effectively manage available resources and ways to monitor their performance, and how to trigger alarms in case of a resource failure or any event.

This chapter will explain the three most crucial and critical aspects of the virtual environments. The chapter begins with gaining understanding of **High Availability (HA)** and getting familiar with its configuration procedures, and then moves forward to **Fault Tolerance (FT)** and **Distributed Resource Scheduler (DRS)**. DRS, Storage DRS, and management of DRS clusters play a very important role in managing the whole data center. Often to reap benefits of the complete infrastructure to its maximum potential, HA and DRS are used together.

In this chapter, we will cover the following topics:

- Understanding HA
- Enabling and configuring HA
- Understanding and configuring FT
- Understanding DRS and Storage DRS
- DRS cluster
- Managing and optimizing DRS clusters
- Using HA and DRS together

Understanding High Availability

With VMware ESXi hosts, multiple server workloads are consolidated to one virtual server, and in case of a breakdown or a server failure, it is important to keep the services running. VMware HA helps the administrator achieve a sense of availability concerning minimum downtime for the servers. HA does not provide 100 percent availability of VMs, but rather provides higher availability by rapidly recovering VMs from failed hosts. HA monitors all ESXi hosts in a cluster, and in case a failure is detected, it automatically restarts the VM on a different host. To ensure this functionality, shared storage is needed.

Once a particular ESXi host has crashed, HA restarts those virtual machines on the remaining ESXi hosts in the failover cluster. It can also monitor virtual machines that run in a virtualized environment for guest operating system failures, which means that if the guest operating system of a VM fails, HA can even restart that VM on another ESXi host in the same high-availability cluster. This process is called vSphere HA VM Monitoring and is configured on cluster level. Once enabled, particular VMs are monitored using VMware Tools by sending and receiving heartbeats. A virtual machine is restarted if:

- VMware Tools is not responding using heartbeat signals anymore in a specified time frame
- No network traffic and storage I/O was generated in the last 120 seconds

If a virtual machine was reset, a screenshot will be stored. In case of an operating system crash, such as **Blue Screen of Death** (**BSOD**) or Kernel panic, the administrator can retrace the reason for the issue. Various options control the behavior of this mechanism, including:

- **Failure interval**: Timeout in seconds after a particular VM is reset
- **Minimum uptime**: Timeframe vSphere HA will wait before monitoring the affected VM
- **Maximum per-VM resets**: Maximum of resets per VM
- **Maximum resets time window**: Time window defining how often VMs can be reset, for example, only every 12 hours

These options can be set per priority level of particular virtual machines. We will cover priority levels later in this chapter. Configuring vSphere HA VM Monitoring is a complex topic that needs to be planned and tested carefully. Especially time and reset thresholds need to be chosen wisely.

To configure vSphere HA VM Monitoring, perform the following steps:

1. Login to vCenter Server using vSphere Web Client.
2. Select the **Cluster** and click **Manage**, **Settings**, and **vSphere HA** located under **Services**.
3. Configure the behavior parameters suiting best to your environment.

HA ensures that the services running in the virtual environment are not hampered and are recovered as soon as possible. However, whenever a virtual machine fails over from one host to another host, the guest OS has to be rebooted.

HA uses the concept of heartbeating to detect host failures and performs migration of VMs accordingly. It does this by placing an agent on each host to maintain a heartbeat with all the other hosts in the cluster; a loss of heartbeat automatically triggers a restart of all affected VMs on the other hosts.

HA also keeps a check on the available resources of different clusters at all times, in order to be sure on which host the VMs need to be moved in case of a host failure. HA depends on the categorization of hosts as primary hosts and secondary hosts; the first five hosts powered on in an HA cluster are considered primary and all other remaining are said to be secondary. Primary hosts are responsible for replicating and maintaining the state of the cluster, and also initiating any failover actions. Every host that joins the cluster needs to communicate to the primary hosts to complete its configuration and setup. If a primary host fails, a new primary host is chosen at random from the pool of secondary hosts. HA needs at least one primary host to be available, in order to perform its operations.

HA detects a host failure when the HA agent on a host stops sending heartbeats to the other hosts in the cluster. A host usually stops sending, or fails to send, heartbeats if it gets isolated from the network, crashes, or becomes completely down due to a hardware failure. Once any of these situations is detected, other hosts in the cluster consider the affected host as failed and the said host declares itself isolated from the network. All VMs on the failed host then successfully restart on other hosts in the cluster. A priority can be set in HA to restart or move hosts, ensuring that critical hosts are taken care of first. This restart policy addresses priority of workloads; there are four settings available:

- Disabled
- Low
- Medium
- High

If HA needs to restart a set of particular virtual machines, the order would be:

1. Agent virtual machines – These are special virtual machines that extend the functionality of ESXI hosts; for example, virus-protection or network filtering
2. High priority VMs
3. Medium priority VMs
4. Low priority VMs

To sum it up, if failover resources are not sufficient, HA ensures that more important workloads are recovered first.

A very critical component of vSphere HA is host isolation. Host isolation rules control how particular ESXi hosts will react once they are unable to communicate with each other. If the HA agent on an ESXi host loses this connection, it will try to ping an isolation address. This isolation address can be configured manually and should be a dedicated, independent host with high availability (quorum). By default, host isolation is declared on HA masters after 5 seconds, and on slaves after 30 seconds. The administrator can configure the isolation behavior per cluster basis; there are three major response types that control isolation:

- **Leave powered on**: The state of the virtual machines is not changed.
- **Shut down**: All virtual machines are shut down using VMware Tools. There is a 5-minute timeout after which VMs are powered off.
- **Power off**: All virtual machines are powered off immediately.

Deciding which response type to choose needs deep knowledge of your infrastructure, applications, and the particular behaviors in case of failures. Make sure to plan and test this scenario in detail.

As mentioned in *Chapter 6, Managing Virtual Storage*, datastores also play a very important role in vSphere HA setups. Enabled by default, datastores are used to check whether the other ESXi cluster nodes can be reached if the connectivity can't be verified using the network. This ensures that a cluster won't split in case of a network issue. It is recommended to use two to five datastores for heartbeats. These datastore are selected by default, but the administrator can also configure dedicated datastores.

Configuring HA

HA can be configured while creating a new cluster or by modification of cluster settings at a later stage, whenever required. To configure HA, following steps need to be followed:

1. Select the desired cluster on which HA needs to be enabled.

2. Go to the **Manage** tab and **Settings**.

3. Under **Services**, click **vSphere HA**.

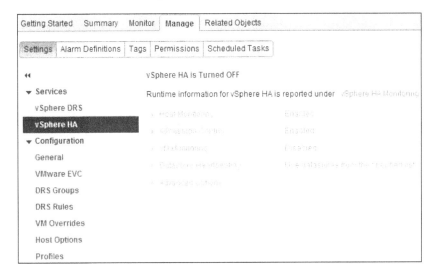

4. Click on the **Edit** button.

5. Select **Turn On vSphere HA**.

The **Host Monitoring Status** section is used to enable the exchange of heartbeats among hosts in the cluster. In order for HA to work, **Host Monitoring** must be enabled. However, it can be disabled temporarily while performing maintenance tasks.

Fault Tolerance

Fault Tolerance is used to protect that virtual machine which requires continuous availability of an application, in the event of a host failure. This is accomplished by creating a live secondary instance of the VM that is in virtual locked state with the primary VM. By allowing instantaneous failover between the two VMs, FT eliminates even the smallest chance of disruption, resulting in zero downtime of the VM.

Functionality

Fault Tolerance makes intensive use of shadowing mechanisms. Once enabled for a particular VM, a secondary VM is created as shadow copy of the original VM. This copy is executed on a different ESXi host and it consumes its own resources such as vCPU, memory, network, and storage. The console of the secondary VM is locked and cannot be used, as all CPU and virtual device inputs on the primary VM are replicated to the secondary VM. This is done using a patented technology called VMware vLockstep. If the primary VM crashes (for example, because of a crash of the ESXi host), the secondary VM, which is an identical replica, immediately takes over. Because all changes inside the virtual machines are synchronized, the guest operating system and applications don't need to be restarted.

FT is compatible with all guest operating systems supported by vSphere, but there are also some exclusions; check out the VMware knowledge base regarding this at `http://kb.vmware.com/kb/1008027`. FT works with HA and DRS for advanced load balancing and optimized initial placement of the virtual machines.

Requirements for FT

On the other hand, Fault Tolerance has also some requirements and disadvantages including:

- vSphere HA must be enabled
- Shared storage is needed
- The virtual machine's virtual disks need to be Thick-provisioned (this limit omitted in vSphere 6.0)
- CPUs must be supported for Fault Tolerance
- ESXi hosts must have compatible processors, preferably the same processor within the same generation
- For vSphere 5.x, only 1 vCPU is supported along with Fault Tolerance, vSphere 6.0 allows up to 2 (Standard, Enterprise) or 4 (Enterprise Plus) vCPUs depending on your vSphere Edition

- Fault Tolerance requires a VMkernel port for shadow transfer. It is preferable to create a dedicated port group for this

Before using VMware Fault Tolerance, it is important to review the Fault Tolerance checklist, which is available in the vSphere documentation center at `https://pubs.vmware.com/vsphere-50/index.jsp?topic=%2Fcom.vmware.vsphere.avail.doc_50%2FGUID-83FE5A45-8260-436B-A603-B8CBD2A1A611.html`

Configuring FT

To enable FT for the desired VM, follow this next procedure:

1. Connect to vCenter Server using vSphere Web Client.

2. Select the desired VM from the inventory.

3. Go to **Actions** pane.

4. Select **All vCenter Actions** and then click **Fault Tolerance**.

5. Click **Turn on Fault Tolerance**.

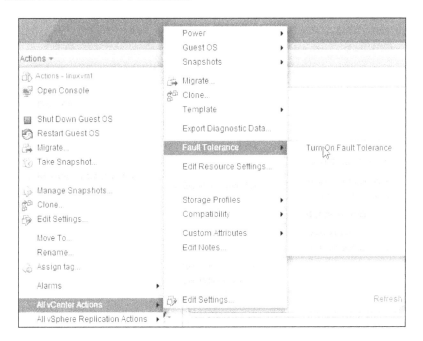

Turning on FT may result in changes in the amount of disk space a VM consumes. After a confirmation, FT will be enabled in a few moments.

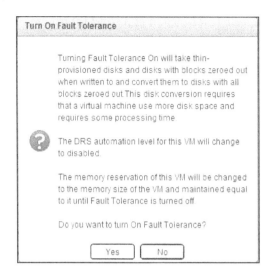

To test Fault tolerance, you can perform a test failover by selecting the VM to be tested and then selecting **Actions | All vCenter Actions | Fault Tolerance | Test Failover**.

As soon as this option is selected, the current machine is migrated from the primary to the secondary virtual machine. The failover takes only a few short moments, resulting in almost zero downtime for the application. As soon as the machine is migrated to a new host, a new secondary virtual machine is generated on a different host for a failover, in case this machine fails. This means that the virtual machine is still in protection by fault tolerance.

Distributed Resource Scheduler (DRS)

DRS continuously monitors utilization across ESXi hosts. It smartly allocates available resources among virtual machines, based on business or resource requirements. DRS is a powerful feature which balances the virtual workloads automatically, in order to effectively manage available resources and eliminate resource contention across configured hosts. DRS makes use of vMotion to optimize resource automation for automatic migration of VMs across hosts in a cluster. Using a feature called initial placement DRS ensures that added virtual machines are placed on a particular ESXi host with the lowest resource utilization. As a result, newly created virtual machine don't affect a DRS cluster's fair resource distribution. DRS can also be configured to manually or partially automate or fully automate for allocating resources as per requirements in different virtual server setups.

DRS utilizes resource pools and clusters that combine the resources of multiple hosts into one single entity. An administrator can also create multiple resource pools to divide the resources of single or multiple hosts into various entities.

When a VM encounters increase in load, DRS checks for its priority against the defined resource allocation rules. If the requirements are met, it allocates the virtual machine among the physical servers to provide them necessary resources, and to eliminate resource contention. After the resources are allocated, vMotion migrates the virtual machine to a different host. The dynamic resource allocation also ensures that the resources are always made available to VMs with higher priority. while simultaneously maximizing overall resource utilization.

Configuring DRS

DRS can be configured in the same way as HA. It can be configured during the cluster creation or whenever required. To configure DRS in your virtualized infrastructure, the mentioned procedure are as follows:

1. Select the desired cluster on which DRS needs to be enabled.

2. Go to the **Manage** tab and **Settings**.

3. Under **Services**, click **vSphere DRS**.

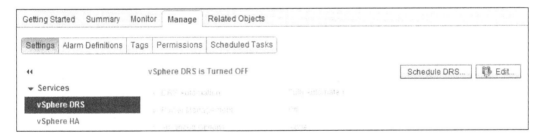

4. Click the **Edit** button.

5. Select **Turn On vSphere DRS**.

You can optionally configure some additional settings to change the way DRS functions. To access these settings, click on the **VMware DRS** item in the Cluster **Settings** window.

Also, we can customize the way DRS performs its operations. It has three basic modes of working which can be switched as per needs. These modes are:

- **Manual**: A VM is initially placed on an ESXi host recommended by DRS, after being approved by the administrator. It is not migrated afterwards; the administrator needs to adjust the VM placement manually.

- **Partially Automated**: VMs are initially placed on ESXi hosts automatically. DRS recommends to migrate workloads if necessary, but the administrator still needs to approve recommendations.

- **Fully Automated**: VMs are placed and migrated automatically, based on DRS recommendations.

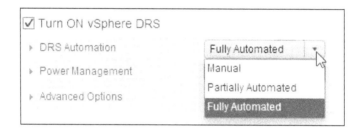

After DRS is successfully enabled, the administrator can monitor it by selecting the cluster in vCenter Server and choosing the **Summary** tab. All the details related to load deviations, the number of faults and recommendations, and the automation level are displayed. By clicking the **Resource distribution chart**, the administrator can also check CPU and memory utilization on a per VM basis, grouped by host.

DRS Cluster

DRS cluster is a group of ESXi hosts and its virtual machines, which shares resources and are managed by the same vCenter Server. A DRS cluster enables cluster level resource management for effective utilization of the resources. Whenever a host is added to a DRS cluster, the cluster acquires the resources of the host and is added to cluster's resource pool and all the cluster wide resource allocation policies and protocols are by-default implemented on the host.

Managing and optimizing DRS Clusters

DRS clusters can be managed using vCenter Server, and following operations can be performed to configure the DRS cluster:

- Adding hosts to the cluster
- Adding virtual machines to the cluster
- Managing power resources for a cluster

Adding a host to the cluster

To add a host to the cluster, perform the following steps:

1. Select the host to be added from the inventory.
2. Drag the host to the target cluster.
3. Select as per need – should a new resource pool be created for the host's virtual machines or can the resources be merged in the cluster's resource pool?

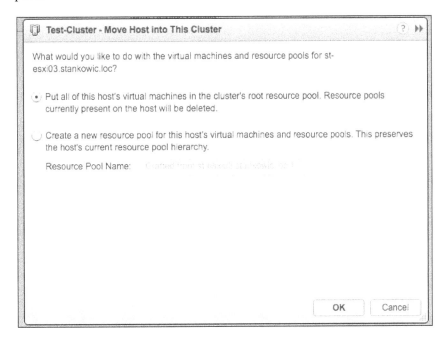

To remove hosts from a cluster, maintenance mode has to be enabled first. We can then drag and move the host to any other cluster or location in the inventory.

Adding virtual machines to the cluster

There are three different ways to add virtual machines to a cluster, which are explained next:

- All virtual machines in a host are, by default, added to the cluster, if the host is added to the cluster

- Virtual machines can be migrated from a host to a cluster, or from a cluster to another cluster using vMotion

- A virtual machine can be added to a cluster while creation, by just selecting the location as the desired cluster

To remove a virtual machine from a cluster, the virtual machine can be migrated from the cluster to another host or cluster; or the host can be removed from the cluster and all virtual machines in it will be moved to the desired location.

Managing power resources in a cluster

Distributed Power Management (DPM) is a component of DRS, which monitors and tracks power requirements of hardware resources. It cuts off or allocates power as per need. DPM can be enabled from **Power Management Settings** under every cluster's settings.

Using HA and DRS together

HA and DRS can be used together for load balancing along with failover. Together, HA and DRS bring out a more effective and balanced cluster, specially when HA initiates migrating its virtual machines to different hosts.

In case of a failover, HA takes control of the situation and restarts all the affected virtual machines on the other hosts. It also makes sure that the critical machines are made available with minimal downtime. Whenever such a situation arises, the hosts get over loaded with extra machines, while some are still functioning with abundant resources available at hand. If DRS is also enabled along with HA, then DRS ensures that it understands, and restarts or moves machines accordingly on different servers, in such a way which ensures smooth operations for all machines.

Storage DRS

Storage DRS enables the administrator to manage the resources of a datastore cluster in the same way the DRS does for a host. Once Storage DRS is enabled, it recommends virtual machine disk placement and migration options to balance space and I/O resources across the datastores in the cluster.

To enable or disable Storage DRS, you can select or deselect the **Enables Storage DRS** option from the **Datastore Cluster Settings** dialog. You can follow the next steps to configure Storage DRS:

1. Login into vCenter using vSphere Web Client.

2. Select the desired datastore cluster.

3. Go to the **Manage** tab and click **Settings**.

4. Under **Services**, click **Storage DRS** and then click **Edit**.

5. Select **Turn On vSphere DRS**.

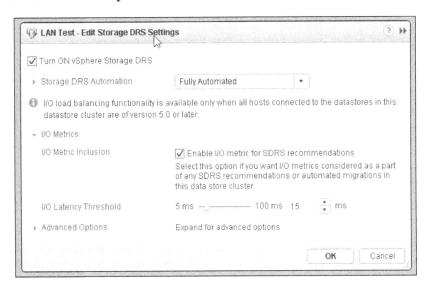

Summary

In this chapter, we covered some of the more popular and advanced features in vSphere. We gained a considerable understanding of High Availability and its configuration procedure. We also learnt how to apply to mission-critical workload's requirements by enabling Fault Tolerance. To ensure fair resource consumption, we also had a look at DRS.

In the next chapter, we will have a look at vSphere patch and update management. To keep our environment secure and updated, we will learn how to patch our ESXi hosts, and keep them secure by configuring firewalls and using additional products including vCloud Networking and Security. To sum it up, we will also learn how to integrate our virtual infrastructure into Microsoft Active Directory and protect our hosts against unpermitted access.

11
Securing and Updating vSphere

In the previous chapter, we learnt how to configure and use HA, FT, and DRS in the VMware environment.

In this chapter, we will discuss the methods and configurations necessary to secure the vSphere architecture from threats. We will also discuss the methods for configuring ESXi firewall. In addition, we will cover security profile services, lockdown mode, AD integration with vSphere, using vCloud Networking and Security.

By the end of this chapter, you will have learnt about the following topics:

- Configuring ESXi firewall
- Understanding security profile services and lockdown mode
- Microsoft Active Directory integration with vSphere
- Using vCloud Networking and Security
- Access controls and configuring roles and permissions
- Installing, configuring and using vSphere Update Manager for patch management
- Maintenance mode

VMware vSphere ESXi includes a firewall between its network and management interface. Whenever an ESXi host is installed, the firewall is enabled by default and is configured with default settings, allowing default services, and blocking other incoming and outgoing traffic. However, the firewall allows ICMP pings and communication services with DHCP and DNS (UDP only) clients.

VMware also offers a very comprehensive guide for hardening virtual infrastructure setups. It is available online at `http://www.vmware.com/security/hardening-guides`.

Each vSphere host has a firewall that is used to protect its management network. There are two ways to manage that host firewall – either by using a vSphere Client, or by using the ESXi command shell to configure firewall using the command line.

Configuring ESXi firewall

To configure the firewall using the vSphere Web Client, follow the steps listed next:

1. Log in to the Web Client and select the vCenter icon.
2. Navigate to the list of hosts and select the desired host.
3. Under **Manage**, select **Settings** and go to **Security Profile**.
4. Configure firewall ports for both incoming and outgoing data for the host, by clicking on the **Edit** button.
5. Select the service you want to enable or disable and make desired changes.

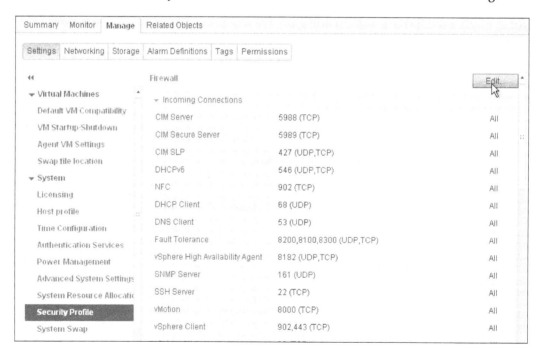

Now we will see how to configure the firewall using the CLI commands using vCLI shell:

1. After logging on the CLI shell, first check the statistics of the firewall using the following command:

    ```
    esxcli network firewall get
    ```

2. By default, the firewall should be enabled. However, to alter the state of firewall, following command is used:

    ```
    esxcli network firewall set -enabled false
    ```

    ```
    esxcli network firewall set -enabled true
    ```

3. Once the firewall is enabled, use the following command to get the list of current firewall rules:

    ```
    esxcli network firewall ruleset list
    ```

4. The administrator can also enable and disable a particular firewall rule with the use of following commands:

    ```
    esxcli network firewall ruleset -enabled true -ruleset-id
    rulesetName
    ```

    ```
    esxcli network firewall ruleset -enabled false -ruleset-id
    rulesetName
    ```

5. In order to restrict IP address range from allowing a particular service or port, following set of commands can be used:

    ```
    esxcli network firewall ruleset allowedip add -ruleset-id
    RulesetName -ip-address IPAddress/Network
    ```

    ```
    esxcli network firewall ruleset allowedip remove -ruleset-id
    RulesetName -ip-address IPAddress/Network
    ```

    ```
    esxcli network firewall ruleset allowedip list -ruleset-id
    RulesetName
    ```

6. Verify the changes with the following command:

    ```
    esxcli network firewall ruleset allowedip list
    ```

7. Once all changes are made, its ideal to refresh the firewall to make sure all changes are in effect:

    ```
    esxcli network firewall refresh
    ```

Understanding security profile services and lockdown mode

VMware ESXi built-in firewall is known as **security profile**. It is the firewall for the entire host including the management interface, but not the virtual guest machines running on the host. We have already learnt how to configure the security profile firewall using vSphere Web Client and the command shell. To ensure central manageability, we can use a feature called lockdown mode through vCenter Server.

Lockdown mode

Lockdown mode is used to restrict a host to be accessed and operated by vCenter Server only, to enhance security. Only `vpxuser` has the authentication, and can perform any operations on the ESXi host directly.

In accordance with vSphere 6.0 latest changes I think it is necessary to add another sentence after this one:

With vSphere 6.0 it is also possible to specify a list of users that are eligible to access the Direct Console User Interface (DCUI). For this, the advanced setting DCUI. `Access` needs to be altered on the ESXi host.

To enable lockdown mode using vSphere Web Client, perform the following steps:

1. Login to vCenter Server using vSphere Web Client.
2. Choose the host in the inventory panel.
3. Click on the **Configuration** tab and select **Security Profile**, which is located in the **System** pane.
4. Click on the **Edit** button next to lockdown mode.
5. Select **Enable Lockdown Mode** and click **OK**.

Lockdown mode can be enabled/disabled using the direct console as well, by using the toggle button which says **Configure Lockdown Mode**. In case vCenter Server is down or the host is disconnected, the option to configure the lockdown is disabled by default.

Microsoft Active Directory integration with vSphere

ESXi hosts can be configured to join a Microsoft Active Directory domain, which enables a user to access the host with the same credentials as his Active Directory domain credentials. If Active Directory is in sync with the vSphere environment, then every time a user is prompted to enter the credentials, Active Directory credentials can be used for authentication purposes, eliminating the need of creating host based local accounts.

This service is very useful in managing large server architectures, and all the user accounts can be centrally managed by Active Directory. This architecture provides more security and also ease to manage accounts independently from the hosts. However, local users can still be created and configured as per requirements using the vSphere Web Client. Root user can not be created or synced with an Active Directory account and needs to be separate at all times.

Using Active Directory for managing user accounts also provides the ability to grant permissions and set rules for every user account. It can be controlled and configured using Active Directory groups.

To configure a host with Active Directory, follow the steps mentioned next:

1. Create an Active Directory group named **ESX Admins** and right-click on the group to add members to it.

    ESX Admins is the default group name. If you prefer to use a different group name, it can be changed from vSphere Web Client from **Advanced System Settings** under the **Manage** tab of the desired host. The setting is named `Config.HostAgent.plugins.hostsvc.esxAdminsGroup`.

2. To join the host to the domain, go to **Settings** under the **Manage** tab on the desired host.

3. Click **Authentication Services**.

4. By default, **Directory Services Type** is set to **Local Authentication**. Click the **Join Domain** button.

5. Enter the domain name and provide the domain admin user credentials to login.

6. The setting **Directory Services Type** will now change to **Active Directory**.

Using vCloud Networking and Security

VMware **vCloud Networking and Security** (**vCNS**) is a security virtual appliance suite that integrates seamlessly with other VMware products, including:

- VMware vCenter Server
- VMware vSphere
- VMware vCloud Directory

It is a crucial security component to protect hosts and data centers from security threats and attacks, and also help the administrator achieve compliance goals. Previously, functions of vCNS were included in a dedicated product called vShield, but beginning with vSphere 5.1 VMware, they became part of the vCloud product suite. Therefore, vCNS cannot be bought as a separate product anymore.

The product offers the following components:

- **vShield Manager**: It is the central management tool that manages all components that are part of the vCNS product.

- **vShield Edge**: vShield Edge installs an appliance acting as network gateway between the virtual data center and the physical infrastructure. It offers plenty of services including virtual firewalls:

    ◦ IPSec: Internet Protocol Security

    ◦ VPN: Virtual Private Network

    ◦ NAT: Network Address Translation

    ◦ VXLAN: Virtual Extensible LAN

    ◦ DHCP: Dynamic Host Configuration Protocol

- **vShield App**: This appliance is a hypervisor-based, application level firewall. It enables the administrator to implement firewalls at vNIC level. It also enables the administrator to create access level control policies, irrespective of the network topology. Beyond that, it also monitors all incoming and outgoing traffic of the ESXi host.

- **vShield App with Data Security**: In addition to vShield App, vShield App with Data Security provides scanning functionality for Microsoft Windows CIFS shares to detect sensitive data such as credit card information. As a result administrators can fulfill regularly compliance audit's requirements.

A product that is also often mentioned along with vCNS is vShield Endpoint. Previously, this was part of the vShield Suite but beginning with vSphere 5.1, it became part of vSphere editions Standard or higher. vShield Endpoint offers endpoint security interfaces. It enables antivirus processing and as a result, allows the administrators to integrate third-party, antivirus solutions in their virtual infrastructure.

With vCNS, administrators are able to improve their virtual infrastructure's security while extending flexibility. For customers interested in implementing big and automating cloud infrastructure setups, vCNS is an essential product.

More detailed information about vCNS can be found on the VMware website at `https://www.vmware.com/de/products/vcloud-network-security`.

Access controls and configuring roles and permissions

Roles are a set of one or more privileges, which allow access to specific tasks and are generally clubbed together with other privileges related to it. List of roles can be viewed from the **Administration | Roles** pane in vSphere Web Client. All roles are equally prioritized and no role is superior or subordinate to another role.

The administrator needs to set up proper access controls to stop virtual machines from being vulnerable to attacks, as any user can delete or modify the guest operation system or make changes to any of the folders. These access controls can be managed and configured using **Roles and Permissions**.

Permissions define the access limitation to the particular object in the inventory. Every object in the inventory has the permissions tab from where it can be managed. Granting permission to any user for any object can be done from the Permissions tab by selecting the **Add Permission** option.

Getting started with vSphere Update Manager

vSphere Update Manager (vUM) is used as a centralied, automated patch and version management. It is intended to be used along with VMware ESX/ESXi hosts and can be used to:

- Apply updates to ESXi hosts
- Upgrade ESXi hosts
- Update virtual machine's VMware Tools software
- Upgrade virtual machine's virtual hardware version
- Update VMware appliances

Unlike other vCenter Server add-ons, vUM is not yet fully integrated into vSphere Web Client. It only offers the possibility to scan ESX/ESXi hosts and list their patch compliance. For using the full feature set, you need to use the vSphere legacy client.

vUM downloads the list of available and relevant patches to your virtual infrastructure from www.vmware.com. This task is executed daily to ensure continuous availability of the most recent patches. Before patching ESXi hosts, patches are staged and virtual machines are moved to other cluster nodes to ensure availability. Using vUM, administrators are also able to verify patch compliance to their virtual infrastructure.

> Note: Update Manager 5.x does not support virtual
> machine patch operations.

vSphere Update Manager requirements

Make sure the following requirements are fulfilled before proceeding to install vUM:

- x86 processor with two or more logical cores and at least 2 GHz clock-rate
- 2 GB memory
- Microsoft Windows Server 2003 or newer
- 32-bit ODBC driver and DSN for external databases
- Sufficient hard disk capacity for patches

Make sure to check VMware Product Interoperability Matrix to ensure that your operating system and database is supported. It can be checked at `http://www.vmware.com/resources/compatibility/sim/interop_matrix.php`.

VMware offers an Microsoft Excel sheet for calculating the storage needs for vUM in your virtual infrastructure. During calculation, the amount of ESXi hosts, ESXi versions, and virtual machines are evaluated. The sheet can be downloaded from `https://pubs.vmware.com/vsphere-60/topic/com.vmware.ICbase/PDF/vsphere-update-manager-60-sizing-estimator.xls`.

It is also possible to use an integrated Microsoft SQL Server 2008 Express Edition as database backend. The appropriate installation files are part of the installation media. Setups with more than 5 hosts and 50 virtual machines require an external database backend.

Installing vSphere Update Manager

vUM is compatible with vCenter Server add-ons like VMware Converter Enterprise for vCenter. It can be installed from the vCenter installation media or it can be downloaded separately, either as an ISO or a ZIP file from the VMware download portal (customer login required).

To install vUM, perform the following steps:

1. Execute the autorun function on the vCenter installation media, click **VMware vSphere Update Manager** and then on the **Install** button.
2. Accept the End-user license agreement (EULA).

3. To download updates after the installation, enable **Download updates from default sources immediately after installation**.

4. Enter the vCenter Server username and password.

5. Select the integrated Microsoft SQL Server 2008 Express Edition or provide a valid 32-bit DSN for an external database.

6. Verify that the displayed networking information matches your system's network interface that has access to ESXi hosts.

7. Enter proxy server settings, if required.

8. Select where vUM should store patches.

9. Click **Install** to start the installation process.

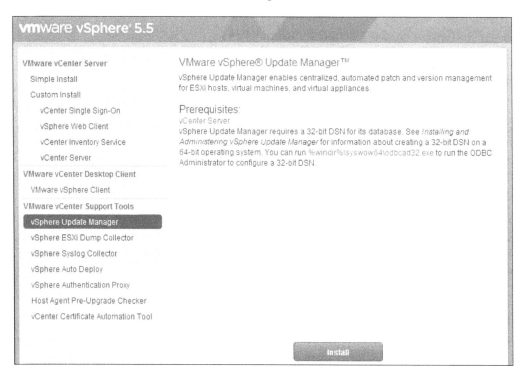

Installation should be complete in the next few minutes. Once vSphere Update Manager is installed, you need to install the client plugin as well. This plugin is required to access vUM.

To install the vUM client plugin, follow the mentioned steps:

1. Start the vSphere legacy client and click **Plug-ins** for the drop-down menu.

2. Click **Download** and Install on the highlighted plugin.

3. After the installation is done, you can see that the plugin is enabled and ready to use. The following screenshot shows the vSphere legacy client plug-in list offering the vUM plug-in for installation:

Plug-in Name	Vendor	Version	Status	Description
Installed Plug-ins				
VMware vCenter Storage Mon...	VMware Inc.	5.5	Enabled	Storage Monitoring and Reporting
vCenter Hardware Status	VMware, Inc.	5.5	Enabled	Displays the hardware status of hosts (CIM monitoring)
vCenter Service Status	VMware, Inc.	5.5	Enabled	Displays the health status of vCenter services
Available Plug-ins				
VMware vSphere Update Ma...	VMware, Inc.	5.5.0....	Download and I...	VMware vSphere Update Manager extension

After the installation, you will see a new button on the home page of the vSphere legacy client, **Update Manager**. Click this icon to configure and use vUM.

It is recommended to verify download scheduling and mail notification settings right after the installation. For this verification, perform the following steps:

1. Login to vCenter Server using the vSphere legacy client.
2. Click **Update Manager**.
3. Click **Configuration**, **Download Schedule**, and **Edit Download Schedule**. Enter your desired download schedule and a valid mail address for reporting downloaded patches.
4. To test downloading patches, switch to the **Download Settings** pane and click **Download Now**.
5. After patches are downloaded, a comprehensive list can be found in the **Patch Repository** pane.

Configuring and using VMware vSphere Update Manager

vUM divides the patches and upgrades them into the following sections:

* **Baselines**: Baselines include one or multiple patches, add-ons, or upgrades
* **Baseline groups**: Baselines can be grouped to baseline groups (for example, driver updates and critical patches)

To enable ESXi host patch management, clusters and ESXi hosts are configured to subscribe particular baselines or baseline groups. To configure vUM to stage and remediate patches, perform the following steps:

1. Login to vCenter Server using the vSphere legacy client.
2. Click **Update Manager** and **Baselines** and **Groups**.
3. Two baselines are created by default: **Critical Host Patches** and **Non-Critical Host Patches**.
4. If you want to group baselines, click **Create** on the **Baseline Groups** pane. An example would be to combine critical and noncritical patches as generic baseline group. To do so, select those baselines in the wizard (Patches section) and click **Finish**.

After baselines and baseline groups are configured, ESXi hosts and clusters can be audited. Follow the next steps to audit:

1. Select a cluster or particular ESXi host from the inventory and click on the **Update Manager** pane.
2. Click **Attach** to attach baselines or baseline groups to the selected cluster or host.
3. Click **Scan** to verify patch compliance status. The following screenshot shows two hosts audited in the vSphere legacy client:

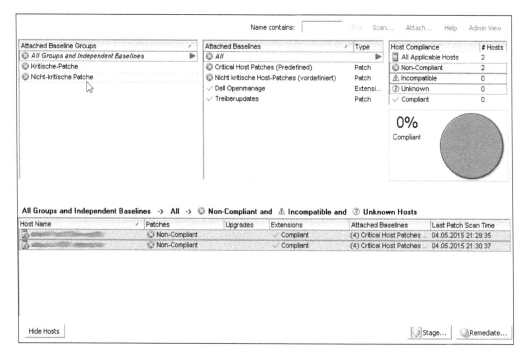

If virtual machines are located on shared storage, ESXi hosts can be patched without shutting down the particular workloads. To remediate clusters and ESXi hosts, proceed with the following steps:

1. Select your cluster and open the **Update Manager** pane.

2. Stage ESXi patches by clicking **Stage** and selecting the patches that should be uploaded to the particular cluster node.

3. Review and acknowledge the particular patches.

4. Click **Remediate** to prepare the patch process. Select the patches that should be installed.

5. Enter a task name and description for documentation purposes.

6. It is also possible to automatically patch the whole cluster including virtual machine migration if you selected a cluster. In the **Cluster Remediation Options** pane, make sure to select **Enable parallel remediation for the hosts in the selected clusters**. You can either let vUM determine the maximum amount of parallel patch processes or define them manually.

7. Finish the wizard and start the patching process.

8. The process can be tracked in the **Recent Tasks** pane of the vSphere legacy client. The screenshot below shows remidiation settings before patching a cluster:

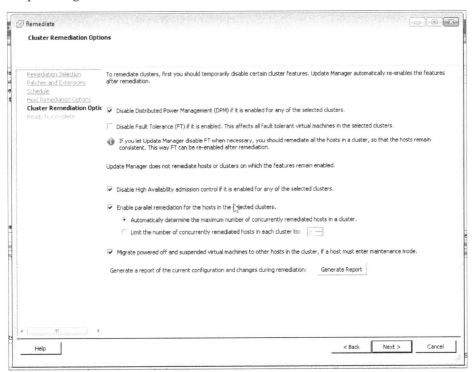

This process needs to be followed many times, since new patches and updates are released frequently.

Using vSphere Update Manager can ensure meeting application's availability demands on one hand, and a secure virtual infrastructure on the other hand. We can execute maintenance tasks without influencing end-users accessing virtual machines on our infrastructure.

Maintenance mode

When DRS maintenance mode is invoked, DRS is used to evacuate all virtual machines from one host to another, without incurring any downtime. This is specially useful for performing maintenance, updating an ESXi host, installing additional memory, or upgrading firmware, and so on.

In order to use maintenance mode in the vSphere architecture, a cluster needs to be created and DRS must be enabled. We have already covered how to create a cluster and enable DRS on the cluster in previous chapters. Once the cluster is created with DRS enabled, add the desired hosts to the cluster.

Once we have the hosts added to the cluster, select the host that needs to go in the maintenance mode. Click **Actions** | **Enter Maintenance** mode. As soon as the administrator confirms the activation of maintenance mode, the virtual machines from this host will be moved using vMotion to other hosts on the same cluster without any downtime. This screenshots demonstrates how to enter maintenance mode for a particular ESXi host using vSphere Web Client:

After the maintenance operations on the said host is complete, we can go to **Actions | Exit Maintenance** mode, to return to normal operations.

Summary

In this chapter, we discussed the methods and configurations necessary to secure the vSphere architecture from threats. We learnt about the basics of ESXi firewall and security profiles available in vSphere architecture, and how and when to implement lockdown mode. Microsoft Active Directory integration enables the administrator to centrally manage the user accounts with ease and flexibility. We also covered the vCloud Networking and Security suite along with its components, and how it protects our virtual infrastructure from threats. We learnt about the various roles and permissions available for objects in the inventory, and how can they be configured. In the end, we saw the use and configuration of vSphere Update Manager and client plugin for the same, along with the maintenance mode for hosts, which enable zero downtime maintenance and patch management.

In the next chapter, we will have a deeper look at vSphere 6.0, the most recent major update of the vSphere product. Especially, we will discuss new technical possibilities to virtualize bigger workloads and also meet I/O-hungry virtual machine's demands. We will also learn how new versions of vCenter Server and vSphere Data Protection can help us more with managing our infrastructure. To sum it up, we will discuss new products that can help customers with utilizing highly available and performant hybrid cloud resources.

12

vSphere 6.0 Overview

This chapter covers the most recent version of the vSphere product. It is important to understand the new features that version 6.0 brings with its release. We will cover how vSphere 6.0 is going to change the **software-defined data centers** (**SDDC**), and will then proceed to take a deeper look at the technical updates that vSphere 6.0 addresses.

Following are the topics we will be discussing in this chapter:

- Introduction to vSphere 6.0
- Scale-up and scale-out applications
- Virtual desktop infrastructure
- NVIDIA GRID vGPU technology
- Instant Clone
- Long-distance vMotion
- Multi-CPU Fault Tolerance
- Content library
- vSphere Web Client
- vCenter Server features and architecture
- Storage capabilities
- vSphere Data Protection
- VMware Integrated OpenStack
- vCloud Air Disaster Recovery

Introduction to vSphere 6.0

VMware defines vSphere as the foundation of Software-defined data centers. For every virtualization and cloud architecture, the end goal is to create a software-defined data center including hybrid clouds. A software-defined data center consists of virtual equivalents for each component of the infrastructure, and is delivered as a service. Every SDDC is controlled and fully automated by software. With vSphere version 6.0, VMware is implementing the same; something which has already been done with storage and network parts of the infrastructure. The end result is a uniform platform, which enables the system administrator to deploy and run data center applications with increased efficiency, while having full control over the data center through software.

vSphere 6.0 supports variations of applications, including existing applications as well as a huge array of new ones. vSphere 6.0 is empowered with many enhancements to address the resource requirements of cloud and data center applications.

Scale-up

With vSphere 6.0, it is now possible to virtualize scale-up applications that were previously considered unvirtualizable, because of their massive scalability or large in-memory database requirements. A well-known example for this kind of application is SAP HANA. Regarding SAP HANA on vSphere, both VMware and SAP published valuable reference documentations:

- VMware SAP virtualization portal: `http://www.vmware.com/go/sap-hana`

- SAP HANA on VMware vSphere Best Practices Guide: `http://www.vmware.com/files/pdf/SAP_HANA_on_vmware_vSphere_best_practices_guide.pdf`

- SAP Note 1788665 – SAP HANA running on VMware vSphere VMs (SAP Service user required): `https://service.sap.com/sap/support/notes/1788665`

vSphere 6.0 offers a new virtual hardware version 11 that has increased scale and configuration maximums to fulfill this requirement. With vSphere 6.0, not only is it possible to virtualize such demanding scale-up applications with no loss in productivity, but also the scale up applications with less resource requirements will inherit performance benefits from it.

A tabular comparison of various upgrades for improving performance in vSphere 6.0 is depicted next:

Upgrade type	vSphere 5.5	vSphere 6.0	Upgrade Size
Virtual Hardware	Version 10	Version 11	
Hosts per cluster	32	64	2x
VMs per cluster	4000	8000	2x
CPUs per host	320	480	1.5x
RAM per host	4 TB	12 TB	3x
VMs per host	512	2048	4x
Virtual CPUs per VM	64	128	2x
Virtual RAM per VM	1 TB	4 TB	4x

Following the upgrade, scale-out applications will see greater consolidation ratios and improved performance, along with larger cluster sizes and greater virtual machine densities.

Scale-out

Just like scale up applications, vSphere 6.0 enable us to virtualize scale-out applications that were earlier considered not virtualizable. Applications like Apache Hadoop/big data Workloads benefit extensively from the vSphere 6.0 enhancements. Increased scale and configuration maximums enable larger cluster sizes, greater consolidation ratios, and improved performance. Apart from vSphere 6.0, VMware offers an add-on called vSphere Big Data Extensions for provisioning and configuring Apache Hadoop clusters. In addition to that, a new feature in vSphere 6.0, Instant Clone, lays the foundation to enable future scale-out applications, including big data workloads, to rapidly clone and deploy VMs. This will enable administrators to deploy virtual machine 10 times faster than before.

vCenter Server features

vCenter Server 6.0 is the first version that offers the same scale numbers for the Windows version as well as the Linux-based Appliance. Previously, customers might have had to choose the Windows variant, when running big virtualized environments. This update enables customers to deploy the version that fits best in their business, without worrying about stability or scalability.

VMware **vSphere Update Manager** (**vUM**) is the only remaining vCenter component that still needs a Windows server. So if you plan to use the vCenter Server appliance, you will still need to install an additional VM, running Microsoft Windows, to provide vUM.

The following table shows the major differences between vCenter Server (Appliance) 6 and 5.5:

Feature	vCS / vCSA 6	vCSA 5.5
Hosts per vCenter	1000	100 (1000 with external Oracle database)
Registered VMs per vCenter	15,000	3000 (10,000 with external Oracle database)
Hosts per cluster	64	32
VMs per cluster	6,000	4,000
Linked Mode	Supported	Not supported

The Windows variant supports a local PostgreSQL installation, limited to 20 hosts and 200 virtual machines, and the following external databases:

- Microsoft SQL Server 2008 R2
- Microsoft SQL Server 2012
- Microsoft SQL Server 2014
- Oracle Database 11g
- Oracle Database 12c

vCenter Server architecture

The vCenter Server design has been consolidated in version 6 to reduce the multitude of components. It now consists of only two major elements:

- vCenter Management Server
- **Platform Services Controller** (**PSC**)

The vCenter Management Server includes management components such as Inventory Service and Web Client. Platform Services Controller consists of essential infrastructure components, which are:

- **Single Sign-On** (**SSO**)
- Central certificate authority
- Licensing registration

With vCenter Server 6, it is possible to split these two services on different hosts. For most environments, it is sufficient to provide PSC embedded into vCS/vCSA. This setup is easy to deploy and manage. The following figure demonstrates the architecture of the vCSA with embdedded PSC:

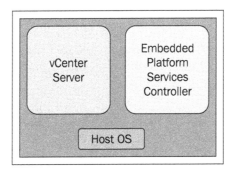

vCenter Server Appliance with embedded PSC.

The following figure shows multiple vCenter Server instances using an external PSC:

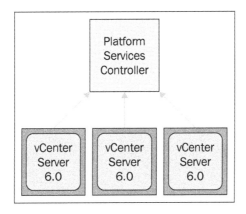

One approach to ensure management availability is to install multiple PSCs and vCenter Servers. Customers can install multiple PSCs and replicate them to ensure that common infrastructure components are available – even in failure scenarios. It is also possible to configure multiple standalone vCenter Servers to use the same PSC. A use case for this scenario is to have multiple dedicated virtual infrastructures inside the same SSO domain. Advanced vSphere technologies, such as VMware Multi-CPU Fault Tolerance and High Availability, help customers to make vCenter Server and its components even more resilient.

Virtual desktop infrastructure

vSphere 6.0 provides extensive power to desktop virtualization. With vSphere 6.0, virtual desktop applications such as VMware Horizon View 6 can use **NVIDIA Virtual Graphics Processing Unit** (**vGPU**) to take advantage of NVIDIA GRID video cards, when present in the host, to display superior 2D and 3D graphics using native NVIDIA GRID drivers. With the use of vGPU, desktop virtualization environments gain efficiency at scale by utilizing the benefits of pooled GPU resources and eliminating the need of 1 to 1 GPU to virtual desktop mappings.

NVIDIA GRID vGPU technology

Using proven desktop virtualization technology, users are able to access their workspace independent of their device. As a result, infrastructure costs can be lowered, while ensuring increased security and higher productivity in comparison to classic PC setups. With vSphere 6.0, VMware offers the GRID vCPU technology in partnership with NVIDIA.

Using this feature set, it is possible to share GPU resources as efficiently and fast as on local computers, to also fulfill graphic intensive application requirements. Graphic commands are passed directly to GPUs without interfering with the hypervisor. NVIDIA Tegra GPU resources are shared between virtual machines to use them more effectively. This enables end users to pick a device of their choice, which reduces device costs.

Previously, virtual desktop's user experience was at times less optimal when running graphic intensive applications, because of inefficient resource sharing.

Instant Clone

Instant Clone is a new feature that was previously developed as **Project Fargo**. It is intended to speed-up massive virtual machine deployments. This especially applies to virtual desktop infrastructures and big data setups. VMware claims that using this technology to deploy hundreds of virtual machines is only a matter of minutes, as it is up to ten times faster than the previous mechanism, which took much longer.

Virtual machines that are instantly cloned, primarily share the disk and memory data with the dependent virtual machine, which reduces the resource usage. Differing disk and memory resources are stored as delta, using a Copy-On-Write mechanism. The following figure explains the difference between Fast Provisioning and the well-known Full Clone mechanism.

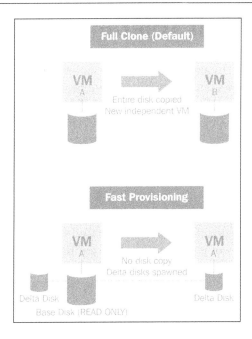

Long-distance vMotion

Hosting virtualized multi-tier applications is a common challenge for vSphere administrators. The need is to have the resources close enough to the end-users, to fulfill speed requirements. On the other hand, another often requested requirement is to spread workloads to alternate computing resources. This is often needed to fulfill complex disaster scenarios requirements to avoid any unplanned downtime.

VMware overhauled its proven vMotion technology to address the following eliminating demands:

- Stretched cluster architectures (metro clustering)
- Hybrid cloud setups
- Multisite load-balancing

This technology allows vMotion operations over network connections with up to 100ms **Round Trip Time (RTT)** latencies. Previous vMotion implementation limited the nondisruptive live migration of running virtual machines to network connections with up to 10ms RTT latency.

For the first time, this enables the customers to migrate workloads between continents in an adequate timely manner.

Multi-CPU Fault Tolerance (SMP-FT)

The number of applications running on a server, require multi vCPU configurations, has grown exponentially. In a recent VMware customer data study, it was found that over 68 percent of the virtual machines have more than one vCPU. This means that current fault tolerance capabilities of one vCPU, used to maximize availability, can not be used on 68 percent of workloads. The cost of unplanned downtime for this class of applications could be devastating. For example, in a typical retail environment, unplanned downtime for a mission-critical application, such as a POS system, could result in losses of up to $1,000 per minute per store, during the peak shopping season.

vSphere 6.0 further innovates on technologies that deliver availability for unplanned downtime. vSphere first introduced software-based fault tolerance in 2009, and now takes it to another level by delivering true continuous availability for larger virtual machines running more than one vCPU. With vSphere 6.0, multi-processor fault tolerance becomes possible for the first time, with support for up to 4 vCPUs. vSphere editions Standard and Enterprise allow customers to use up to 2 vCPUs along with Fault Tolerance. To use up to 4 vCPUs, it is sufficient to have the Enterprise Plus edition. As a result, Multi-CPU Fault Tolerance now supports all three types of storage provisioning: Thick eager-zeroed, thick lazy-zeroed, and thin-provisioned. Previously, thick eager-zeroed was the only supported provisioning type. Another great benefit is that FT-enabled virtual machines can now be backed up using the vSphere Storage API, which enables workloads to be protected agentless, using products such as vSphere Data Protection.

Content library

Customers using more than one VMware vCenter Server installation on multiple sites often had problems with managing VM templates, scripts, and ISO templates. As previous vCenter Server implementations had no synchronization mechanisms for these data, customers had the challenge to implement their own convenient way for content replication (for example, NFS repositories). Only customers who were using vCloud Suite were able to create the so called catalogs, using vCloud Connector. The main disadvantage was that such implementations required inefficient third-party solutions, outside vSphere.

Content library simplifies management of virtual data center content by offering a central solution. It is now possible to maintain VM templates and ISO templates in centralized catalogs. A main catalog including these files is replicated to subscribed vCenter Server systems, cloning the data to their local catalog. This mechanism also includes a version control system to enable older content to be deleted automatically. To save valuable network bandwidth during company working hours, it is also possible to schedule synchronizations at noncritical timeframes (for example, at night). The following figure demonstrates the workflow that applies to multiple vCenter Server installations along with vSphere Content Library:

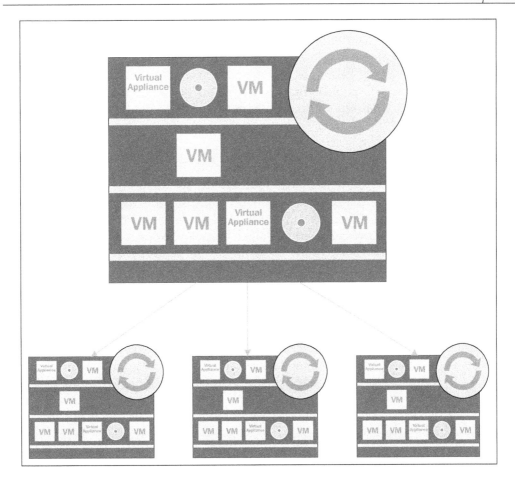

vSphere Web Client

vSphere Web Client is intended to be the next-generation client, superseding the classic vSphere Client. vSphere 6 comes with an updated version of the vSphere Web Client, addressing customer's feedback that VMware had received in numerous satisfaction surveys. These enhancements make the new user interface more responsive, more efficient to navigate, and more intuitive to use. In comparison with previous vSphere Web Client implementations, the most recent version offers:

- 5x faster user-interface responses
- 13x faster login processes
- 4x faster context menus
- Particular actions at minimum 50 percent faster speed

Beyond that, it is now easier to find tasks, menus, and related context to given tasks. To customize the user interface look and feel, it is possible to drag and drop the particular components. As the new Web Client's workflow looks more like the well-known vSphere Client now, it is easier for customers to migrate. Finally, VMware names that the updates vSphere Web Client is the first release which is fully comparable with the well-known legacy vSphere client.

Storage in vSphere 6.0

With vSphere 6.0, VMware makes its entry to the storage market. Especially, the hypervisor and virtual architecture of vSphere 6.0 implements the opportunity to address raising challenges in the storage industry. The hypervisor is appropriately placed in the infrastructure stack, and has the ability and control to make decisions pertaining to the demands of virtual applications, with the supply of underlying infrastructure.

vSphere 6.0 aims to transform storage, bring operational efficiency, and improve virtual infrastructure computing capabilities. Virtualizing storage resources into logical virtual machine centric pools of capacity, which can be flexibly consumed, is the add-on from the vSphere 6.0 to the available storage systems. Also, with the new vSphere, automation of delivery of storage service levels to applications through a standard protocol based approach remains common across all tiers of storage.

Virtual Volumes

VMware introduces **vSphere Virtual Volumes** (**VVOLs**), a new framework of abstraction for external storage (SAN and NAS) devices. Virtual Volumes transforms external storage technology servicing virtualized environments by eliminating longstanding, rigid physical constructs and creating flexible VM-centric datastores. These VM-centric datastores enable dynamic storage class of service automation and finer control over the native data services of the external storage array.

Basically, external storage arrays become aware of the VM architecture, and traditional storage operations such as snapshots, clones, and replications can be performed on a per VM basis. This brings increase in operational efficiency for virtualized data centers.

VVOLs is an industry-wide initiative that will allow customers to leverage the unique capabilities of their current storage investments, and transition without disruption to a simpler and more efficient operational model optimized for virtual environments, that works across all storage types.

Major storage vendors participated in the design of VVOLs. It can be assumed that many other vendors will also support the initiative by adopting implementations.

vSAN All-Flash

Since its introduction in vSphere 5.5, VMware **Virtual SAN (vSAN)** has fast become a cost-effective alternative to conventional storage arrays for virtual data centers. To address the Software Defined Shared-Storage philosophy, local storage devices, connected to ESXi hosts are used cluster-wide as mirrored data stores. Beginning with vSphere 6.0, VSAN now supports two completely different operating modes. As a result, customers can enable their virtual infrastructure to also fulfill very IO lasting application requirements:

- **Hybrid mode**: Using SSD storage as cache and hard drives as datastores
- **All-Flash mode**: Using SSD storage as cache as well as datastores

As a result, VSAN All-Flash enables customers to virtualize more IO heavy workloads. Refer to the following table to see performance differences between different VSAN implementations:

Upgrade type	VSAN 5.5	VSAN 6 All-Flash	Upgrade Size
Hosts per cluster	32	64	2x
VMs per host	100	200	2x
IOPS per host	20.000	90.000	4.5x
Snapshots per VM	2	32	16x
vDisk size	2 TB	62 TB	31x

VSAN 6 offers rack-awareness intelligence, which places more intelligent storage replicas to avoid data loss forced by faulted server racks. To implement this feature, particular ESXi hosts are grouped into fault domains. IIn combination with storage policies, it is possible to have better control about tolerated faults. As a result, customers are eligible to protect mission-critical workloads. Ensuring this infrastructure's resilience, a monitoring for all VSAN-related components, including ESXi hosts, storage hardware, and network status, has been implemented. This helps vSphere administrators to verify their virtual infrastructure's health state.

vSphere Data Protection

VMware consolidated vSphere Data Protection editions that were available previously. With vSphere 6, all customers having a valid Standard, Enterprise, or Enterprise Plus subscription are eligible to use the Linux-based backup appliance. The product enables to provide up to 8 TB of storage, deduplicated by proven EMC Avamar technology. Another benefit of using the most recent product version is that it comes with agents for Microsoft products, including:

- Microsoft SQL Server (also clusters)
- Microsoft Exchange
- Microsoft Sharepoint

These agents are making it easier to backup the virtual machines running the applications mentioned above more efficient and reliable. During restore tasks, it is possible to select particular SQL databases or exchange boxes, instead of restoring the whole virtual machine. Using this, customers have the ability to reduce restore times.

Using Offsite storage, it is also possible to store backups in remote sites to satisfy complex disaster recovery requirements. Backup's integrity can be checked automatically to ensure always having valid restore possibilities. During this verification process, a backup is restored in a separated virtual machine, before starting the virtual machine. If the virtual machine has booted successfully, it is deleted after VMware Tools functionality is verified. Restoring virtual machines now also works even if vCenter Server is not available. Customers using EMC Data Domain storage systems will benefit from enhanced DD Boost support to increase backup efficiency.

VMware Integrated OpenStack (VIO)

Customers have the choice to build their cloud environments with a fully integrated VMware stack or with open source frameworks such as OpenStack.

VMware has opened connections to serve as the basis for building customized cloud environments, including open source clouds. OpenStack based clouds are only as good as the underlying components that power them, and VMware has made vSphere not only compatible, but optimized for OpenStack through core integrations in a product offering called VMware Integrated OpenStack. VMware Integrated OpenStack is an add-on package that enables organizations to rapidly deploy OpenStack on VMware technologies. It supports the full vSphere portfolio, including:

- vSAN
- NSX

- Storage Policies
- VVOLs
- vRealize Operations Manager
- vRealize Log Insight

This provides best-of-breed components for deploying, managing, and running OpenStack Infrastructure. The product consists of an appliance that provides all the necessary OpenStack components already preconfigured for use with vSphere. These components are:

- Horizon (web user-interface)
- Nova (computing management)
- Cinder (block storage infrastructure)
- Glance (image catalog)
- Neutron (networking management)

Customers having a valid vSphere (with Operations Management) Enterprise Plus or vCloud Suite subscription will receive the product at no extra costs. Apart from that, production support needs to be bought separately per CPU basis. The VMware support covers the vSphere components as well as OpenStack, through a single support contract.

VIO consists of the OpenStack code, preconfigured to use the VMware OpenStack drivers and the tools required to install, upgrade, and operate an OpenStack cloud on top of VMware technologies. It is easy to install, but at the same time leverages powerful VMware-optimized production grade architecture. In addition to VIO, In addition to VIO, VMware is also working on making VMware's enterprise grade tools more OpenStack aware. As a result, customers will be able to use open-source frameworks along with their virtual infrastructure.

vCloud Air Disaster Recovery

vCloud Air is a public cloud platform built on the trusted foundation of vSphere, compatible with your on-premises data center. It includes dedicated infrastructure resources, disaster recovery, and also applications as service offerings. vCloud Air allows you to extend your workloads into the cloud with ease.

As mentioned earlier, it is extremely important to protect applications from downtime. vMotion and Fault Tolerance are significant local availability enhancements, but in case of a catastrophe, it is important to have a disaster recovery plan in place as well. With vSphere 6.0, Disaster Recovery to cloud services will be available.

Specifically, users will be able to, for the first time, failover and failback data and workloads to and from VMware vCloud Air, utilizing vSphere replication. Furthermore, multipoint in time recovery offers flexibility and choice with respect to recover point objectives (RPO). Disaster Recovery to the Cloud services reduces the burden of having to maintain a secondary site in case of emergency situations. The following figure displays how vCloud Air can be integrated in your virtual environment to provide recovery resources:

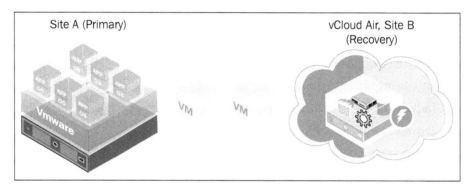

To benefit from this design concept, warm standby capacities are located on vCloud Air resources. Failover and failback workflows are given per virtual machine basis. Customers are able to configure, manage, and administrate their resources using a user-friendly self-service interface.

Summary

In this chapter, we introduced the latest vSphere product update from VMware. vSphere 6.0 is new and very feature rich, enabling customers to virtualize bigger workloads with better management possibilities. To sum it up, vCenter Server Appliance and vSphere Web Client have been massively overhauled to give customers faster and user-friendly utilities for managing their virtual infrastructure. For the first time, vCSA is in no way inferior to the classic Microsoft Windows counterpart, giving customers the free choice of both architectures. It seems like vCSA is fast becoming the primary platform for vCenter Server; so it will definitely be interesting to see how VMware is going to improve this in the future.

To virtualize bigger workloads, including applications such as SAP HANA, VMware updated the virtual hardware version (vHW), enabling more virtual CPUs and memory. I/O intensive workloads can benefit from Virtual SAN 6, which now also supports SSD-only setups to provide even more I/O performance. In comparison with VSAN 5.5, I/O performance can be up to 4.5 times higher.

To fulfill customers' requirements on efficiently using and managing hybrid cloud resources, vSphere 6.0 comes with two major features: VMware Integrated OpenStack (VIO) and Long-distance vMotion. VIO gives customers the possibility to build OpenStack cloud infrastructures based on the full VMware stack. On the other hand, Long-distance vMotion offers the ability to migrate workloads between whole continents, just like in local data centers. This is a massive improvement that fits perfectly into hybrid cloud setups. With vCloud Air Disaster Recovery, customers are able to use dedicated cloud infrastructure resources as cost-effective recovery resources. With vSphere 6.0, VMware also overhauled its own backup and recovery solution, vSphere Data Protection. For the first time, it offers up to 8 TB of deduplicated storage without additional licenses. Interoperability with Microsoft products has been improved by offering agents for applications, including Microsoft SQL Server and Microsoft Exchange. These agents provide a seamless integration to enable backup and restore of particular databases and mailboxes.

To sum it up, vSphere 6.0 includes plenty of great features that help customers use their virtual infrastructure in a more effective and efficient way. Providing resource-hungry workloads was never easier before.

Index

Thank you for buying
VMware vSphere Essentials

About Packt Publishing

Packt, pronounced 'packed', published its first book, *Mastering phpMyAdmin for Effective MySQL Management*, in April 2004, and subsequently continued to specialize in publishing highly focused books on specific technologies and solutions.

Our books and publications share the experiences of your fellow IT professionals in adapting and customizing today's systems, applications, and frameworks. Our solution-based books give you the knowledge and power to customize the software and technologies you're using to get the job done. Packt books are more specific and less general than the IT books you have seen in the past. Our unique business model allows us to bring you more focused information, giving you more of what you need to know, and less of what you don't.

Packt is a modern yet unique publishing company that focuses on producing quality, cutting-edge books for communities of developers, administrators, and newbies alike. For more information, please visit our website at www.packtpub.com.

About Packt Enterprise

In 2010, Packt launched two new brands, Packt Enterprise and Packt Open Source, in order to continue its focus on specialization. This book is part of the Packt Enterprise brand, home to books published on enterprise software – software created by major vendors, including (but not limited to) IBM, Microsoft, and Oracle, often for use in other corporations. Its titles will offer information relevant to a range of users of this software, including administrators, developers, architects, and end users.

Writing for Packt

We welcome all inquiries from people who are interested in authoring. Book proposals should be sent to author@packtpub.com. If your book idea is still at an early stage and you would like to discuss it first before writing a formal book proposal, then please contact us; one of our commissioning editors will get in touch with you.

We're not just looking for published authors; if you have strong technical skills but no writing experience, our experienced editors can help you develop a writing career, or simply get some additional reward for your expertise.

VMware vSphere 5.x Datacenter Design Cookbook

ISBN: 978-1-78217-700-5   Paperback: 260 pages

Over 70 recipes to design a virtual datacenter for performance, availability, manageability, and recoverability with VMware vSphere 5.x

1   Innovative recipes, offering numerous practical solutions when designing virtualized datacenters.

2   Identify the design factors—requirements, assumptions, constraints, and risks—by conducting stakeholder interviews and performing technical assessments.

3   Increase and guarantee performance, availability, and workload efficiency with practical steps and design considerations.

VMware vSphere 5.1 Cookbook

ISBN: 978-1-84968-402-6   Paperback: 466 pages

Over 130 task-oriented recipes to install, configure, and manage various vSphere 5.1 components

1.   Install and configure vSphere 5.1 core components.

2.   Learn important aspects of vSphere such as administration, security, and performance.

3.   Configure vSphere Management Assistant(VMA) to run commands/scripts without the need to authenticate every attempt.

Please check **www.PacktPub.com** for information on our titles

VMware ESXi Cookbook

ISBN: 978-1-78217-006-8   Paperback: 334 pages

Over 50 recipes to master VMware vSphere administration

1. Understand the concepts of virtualization by deploying vSphere web client to perform vSphere administration.

2. Learn important aspects of vSphere including administration, security, performance, and configuring vSphere Management Assistant (VMA) to run commands and scripts without the need to authenticate every attempt.

3. VMware ESXi 5.1 Cookbook is a recipe-based guide to the administration of VMware vSphere.

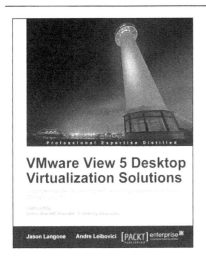

VMware View 5 Desktop Virtualization Solutions

ISBN: 978-1-84968-112-4   Paperback: 288 pages

A complete guide to planning and designing solutions based on VMware View 5

1. Written by VMware experts Jason Langone and Andre Leibovici, this book is a complete guide to planning and designing a solution based on VMware View 5.

2. Secure your Visual Desktop Infrastructure (VDI) by having firewalls, antivirus, virtual enclaves, USB redirection and filtering and smart card authentication.

Please check **www.PacktPub.com** for information on our titles

CPSIA information can be obtained
at www.ICGtesting.com
Printed in the USA
JSHW052306100523
41553JS00002B/55

9 781784 398750